SOURCES AND DOCUMENTS IN THE
HISTORY OF ART SERIES

H. W. JANSON, *Editor*

F. X. Messerschmidt, Grimacing Self-Portrait, *c. 1780,*
Oesterreichische Galerie, Vienna

Neoclassicism and Romanticism

1750-1850

SOURCES and DOCUMENTS

Volume I
Enlightenment/Revolution

Lorenz Eitner

Stanford University

PRENTICE-HALL, INC.
Englewood Cliffs, New Jersey

To Trudi Eitner

PRENTICE-HALL INTERNATIONAL, INC., *London*
PRENTICE-HALL OF AUSTRALIA, PTY. LTD., *Sydney*
PRENTICE-HALL OF CANADA, LTD., *Toronto*
PRENTICE-HALL OF INDIA (PRIVATE) LTD., *New Delhi*
PRENTICE-HALL OF JAPAN, INC., *Tokyo*

Preface

The following selection of documents and literary sources attempts to give a picture of the world of art in the period which began with Winckelmann and ended with Baudelaire. Equivalent to the active life-spans of four generations of artists, the years from 1750 to 1850 comprised two distinct eras, the one leading to, the other descending from Revolution. The great changes which were then about to transform the world affected every sphere of art. Movements and countermovements arose in rapid succession, the artists vacillated between innovation and nostalgia for the past, and their institutions rapidly passed through stages of reform, overthrow, and revival.

In the arts, no less than in politics, the age produced an abundance of theoretical speculation, polemic, and dogma. Surrounded by general change, art itself had become problematical. The shadow of doubt fell on its purpose, its rules and standards, and its relationship with beauty, morality, and nature. Where formerly common sense and routine had seemed sufficient, criticism now found open questions. But much of the discussion which came to center around art reflected in fact other, more general concerns. To the distress of artists, an ever-increasing number of laymen invaded their world, to criticize and speculate.

In making my selection, I have given preference to those writings which seemed to me to have a direct relevance to art itself, to its actual practice and physical reality, rather than to the philosophical debates about it. Much art, even in an argumentative period, enters the world quietly and leaves no literary record. A documentary anthology bound, to favor the eloquent doctrinaire over the silent practitioner, can hardly avoid giving a biased view of the true situation. It is wise to use caution in judging the influence of pure theory on art, and to remember that the more mundane or practical problems which confronted artists—matters of money, position, patronage, and training—usually weighed more heavily on them than matters of doctrine. I have tried to keep some balance in this regard, but am aware that, by giving prominence to the large issues, I have slighted many smaller circumstances which, in their sum, were probably of equal importance.

In grouping the selected texts, I have chosen an historical, rather than topical, sequence which continues without interruption through both volumes of this book. The four main chapters, two of them contained in this first, the other two in the following volume, represent four distinct periods, or generation-spans, within which various strains of ideology appear together, in mutual interaction. Each of the periods had a peculiar character of its own which expressed itself in various forms. Instead of isolating and tracing one by one the separate strands of ideology which ran through them, I have chosen to characterize the periods themselves, and to treat the different ideas which each produced as manifestations of a common historical situation. As a result, the labels of "classicist" or "romantic" under which the ideological factions of the time are usually grouped are not so prominent in the following pages as the title of the book might lead readers to expect, nor do these labels govern the arrangement of the text. In the quoted passages, Romanticism and Classicism appear, rather, as constantly changing, alternative expressions of states of thought and feeling which are tied to periods, rather than to doctrines. By leaving the documents in the context of their time, rather than forcing them into schematic alignments, I have tried to preserve something of their original freshness and competitive energy. Read together, the writings of supposedly antagonistic contemporaries will be found to show hidden affinities: the year of an artist's or writer's birth often tells more about him than the party label he bears.

The translations used in this and the following volume, unless credited to other authors in the accompanying footnotes, are my own. The footnotes contain the essential bibliography. The Index gives concise identifications and dates of individuals merely named in the text.

For help and advice received in the preparation of this book, I am warmly grateful to Miss Janet Byrne, of the Metropolitan Museum, and to Dr. Kurt Forster, Mrs. Jean Kennedy, Dr. Dwight Miller, Mrs. Inga Tarshis, and Mrs. Jean Van Winkle, all of Stanford University. A research grant by the Carnegie Corporation of New York materially furthered my work, and is hereby gratefully acknowledged.

LORENZ EITNER

Contents

I

Enlightenment

INTRODUCTION

In describing the intellectual climate of his time, the philosopher and mathematician d'Alembert (1717–1783) wrote of a "lively fermentation of minds which, spreading through nature in all directions like a river bursting its dams, has violently swept along everything in its way . . . from the principles of the natural sciences to the foundations of revealed religion, from metaphysics to taste, from music to morals, from theological disputes to questions of trade, from the laws of princes to those of peoples: everything has been discussed, analyzed, or at least brought up" (1758).[1] The ferment which d'Alembert observed accompanied the decline of an old order and the emergence of a new state of society. The fateful inevitability of this process was not then apparent to the men who, like d'Alembert, directly participated in it. To them, it seemed to be a deliberate effort of reform, directed against dangerous survivals from the dark past, the rubbish of decaying political and religious establishments, and the superstitions which had for too many centuries enslaved mankind. Their ideal was a renewal of society through the application of scientific methods and a return to moral health, in other words, through reason and nature, twin aspects of one great reality before which the old errors would vanish like a dream. The program which was to bring about this secular salvation was conceived in utilitarian and social terms. It rested on the optimistic assumption that careful planning, general education, and improved institutions could produce a universal advance. The reformers envisioned an ideal society which would function with the regularity and predictability of a vast machine, working in harmony with the even greater mechanism of nature.

The transformation which d'Alembert witnessed was bound to affect art, by changing the atmosphere in which it existed, the economic base on which it rested, the institutions which sustained and regulated it, and the minds of artists and public. The documents which follow illustrate the condition of the arts in the period of the Enlightenment. They have been arranged in such a way as to bring out three characteristic aspects: a guiding idea—the imitation of Antiquity; an exemplary institution—the Academy; and a representative individual—the lay critic of art.

---

[1] J. leRond d'Alembert, *Elements de Philosophie*, I, *Mélanges de litterature, d'histoire et de philosophie*, Amsterdam, 1758, IV, 1.

ANTIQUITY

The belief in the perfectibility of man and the general progress of the human race, two notions deeply imbedded in the ideology of the Enlightenment, needed the support of history: it was important to be able to look back to the reality of a Golden Age in the past to feel confidence in the promise of a future Utopia. Antiquity provided the example of a state of humanity so exalted that a future worth striving for could be conceived in its image. This gave the movement of progress a concrete goal, and it suggested, at the same time, a practical method for reaching it: the systematic study and imitation of Antiquity, that historical moment of human perfection which, having once before been realized, could be attained again, though it was not likely to be surpassed. The belief in the superiority of the Ancients became, in the minds of some, a substitute for a guiding religious faith. It was a rational enthusiasm, supported by the evidence of history, literature, and art, rather than by supernatural authority. This evident agreement with terrestrial reality gave it a special attraction; to follow the example of the Greeks was to find harmony in nature, but in a nature ennobled by reason. In the search for the true spirit of Antiquity, the study of ancient art inevitably played an important role, for art furnished not only the essential documents, it offered models for emulation. In art, the lesson of Antiquity could be most closely read, and most directly applied. Archaeological discovery and the history of ancient art therefore caught the interest of a large lay audience. The excavations at Herculaneum (begun in 1737) and at Pompeii (begun in 1748), and the writings of Winckelmann had an influence which rapidly went beyond the study and the studio, and was soon felt in many fields of practical application, from the planning of towns to the designing of furniture.

Johann Joachim Winckelmann (1717–1768)

"The news of Winckelmann's death struck us like a bolt from the blue, I still remember the spot where I heard the news." [2] *With these words Goethe recalled, many years later, the shock which was felt throughout Europe when Winckelmann was murdered. The career which was brought to an end by a common assassin, at an inn in Trieste, had been one of the*

---

[2] J. W. Goethe, *Dichtung und Wahrheit*, I, in *Goethes Werke* (Sophien Ausgabe), Weimar, 1896, I Abtheilung, XXVII, 184.

most spectacular of the period. It had led in a steep rise from the provincial obscurity of Stendal, in Prussia, where Winckelmann was born as the son of a shoemaker, through the confinement of theological and philological studies, and the meagerness of a schoolmaster's life in the backwoods of Protestant Germany, to a position of high distinction in the Papal city and to eminence in the world of letters. Along the way, Winckelmann had served as librarian to the historiographer of the Holy Roman Empire, Count Bünau at Nöthnitz, in Saxony, and taken advantage of the nearness of Dresden to study the royal collections, guided by the painter Oeser who was later to perform a similar service for Goethe. Throughout these early years, Winckelmann's practical acquaintance with works of ancient sculpture remained small; it is remarkable that he should have drawn from so limited a source the courage to become a polemical author, and some of the insights which enabled him in later years, when he found himself among the rich collections of Rome, to write the first systematic history of ancient art. His early pamphlet Thoughts on the Imitation of Greek Works in Painting and Sculpture *(1755) was written in Dresden, before he had seen Rome or had come face to face with an original work of Greek art, except for coins, gems, and vases. The pamphlet is an attack on the civilization of the Rococo; the picture of a beautiful humanity which it paints is meant to offer the sharpest possible contrast to 18th century reality. It is as revolutionary in its ultimate implications as Rousseau's fantasy of a primitive state of natural virtue. To accept Winckelmann's advice on the imitation of the Greeks was to affirm the need for radical change; there was no comfortable road from Rococo Dresden to the elevation, beauty, and pagan nudity of the Ancients. Winckelmann's vision of Greek art, drawn from intuition and vast reading, rather than direct observation, had the intensity of daydream. It was this wishful ideality which gave to his first book its special force, lifted it above the plodding antiquarianism of the scholars, and brought it to the attention of educated laymen throughout Europe. That he intended to reach this wide audience is evident from the deliberate elegance and vigor of his style which has little in common with the professorial jargon of the period. The following excerpts from Henry Fuseli's translation (London, 1765) preserve the sound of Winckelmann's language better than the more recent renderings.*[3]

---

[3] *Reflections on the Painting and Sculpture of the Greeks . . . Translated from the German Original of the Abbe Winckelmann* by Henry Fuseli, A.M., London, 1765, pp. 1 ff.

From *Thoughts on the Imitation of Greek Works in Painting and Sculpture*
(1755)

I. Nature

There is but one way for the moderns to become great, and perhaps unequalled; I mean, by imitating the ancients. And what we are told
of *Homer,* that whoever understands him well, admires him, we find no
less true in matters concerning the ancient, especially the Greek arts. But
then we must be as familiar with them as with a friend, to find Laocoon
as inimitable as *Homer.* By such intimacy our judgment will be that of
Nicomachus: Take these eyes, replied he to some paltry critic, censuring
the Helen of Zeuxis, *Take my eyes, and she will appear a goddess.*

With such eyes *Michael Angelo, Raphael,* and *Poussin,* considered
the performances of the ancients. They imbibed taste at its source; and
Raphael particularly in its native country. We know, that he sent young
artists to Greece, to copy there, for his use, the remains of antiquity.

It is not only *Nature* which the votaries of the Greeks find in their
works, but still more, something superior to nature; ideal beauties, brain-
born images, as *Proclus* says.

The most beautiful body of ours would perhaps be as much inferior
to the most beautiful Greek one, as Iphicles was to his brother Hercules.
The forms of the Greeks, prepared to beauty, by the influence of the
mildest and purest sky, became perfectly elegant by their early exercises.
Take a Spartan youth, sprung from heroes, undistorted by swaddling-
clothes; whose bed, from his seventh year, was the earth, familiar with
wrestling and swimming from his infancy; and compare him with one of
our young Sybarites, and then decide which of the two would be deemed
worthy, by an artist, to serve for the model of a Theseus, an Achilles, or
even a Bacchus. The latter would produce a Theseus fed on roses, the
former a Theseus fed on flesh, to borrow the expression of *Euphranor.*

The grand games were always a very strong incentive for every
Greek youth to exercise himself. Whoever aspired to the honours of these
was obliged, by the laws, to submit to a trial of ten months at Elis, the
general rendezvous; and there the first rewards were commonly won by
youths, as *Pindar* tells us. *To be like the God-like Diagoras,* was the fond-
est wish of every youth.

Behold the swift Indian outstripping in pursuit the hart: how briskly
his juices circulate! how flexible, how elastic his nerves and muscles! how
easy his whole frame! Thus *Homer* draws his heroes, and his Achilles he
eminently marks for "being swift of foot."

By these exercises the bodies of the Greeks got the great and manly Contour observed in their statues, without any bloated corpulency. The young Spartans were bound to appear every tenth day naked before the Ephori, who, when they perceived any inclinable to fatness, ordered them a scantier diet; nay, it was one of *Pythagoras*'s precepts, to beware of growing too corpulent; and, perhaps for the same reason, youths aspiring to wrestling-games were, in the remoter ages of Greece, during their trial, confined to a milk diet.

They were particularly cautious in avoiding every deforming custom; and *Alcibiades,* when a boy, refusing to learn to play on the flute, for fear of its discomposing his features, was followed by all the youth of Athens.

In their dress they were professed followers of nature. No modern stiffening habit, no squeezing stays hindered Nature from forming easy beauty; the fair knew no anxiety about their attire, and from their loose and short habits the Spartan girls got the epithet of Phænomirides.

Those diseases which are destructive of beauty, were moreover unknown to the Greeks. There is not the least hint of the small-pox, in the writings of their physicians; and *Homer,* whose portraits are always so truly drawn, mentions not one pitted face. Venereal plagues, and their daughter the English malady, had not yet names.

And must we not then, considering every advantage which nature bestows, or art teaches, for forming, preserving, and improving beauty, enjoyed and applied by the Grecians; must we not then confess, there is the strongest probability that the beauty of their persons excelled all we can have an idea of?

Art claims liberty: in vain would nature produce her noblest offsprings, in a country where rigid laws would choke her progressive growth, as in Egypt, that pretended parent of sciences and arts: but in Greece, where, from their earliest youth, the happy inhabitants were devoted to mirth and pleasure, where narrow-spirited formality never restrained the liberty of manners, the artist enjoyed nature without a veil.

The Gymnasies, where, sheltered by public modesty, the youths exercised themselves naked, were the schools of art. These the philosopher frequented, as well as the artist. *Socrates* for the instruction of a Charmides, Autolycus, Lysis; *Phidias* for the improvement of his art by their beauty. Here he studied the elasticity of the muscles, the ever varying motions of the frame, the outlines of fair forms, or the Contour left by the young wrestler on the sand. Here beautiful nakedness appeared with such a liveliness of expression, such truth and variety of situations, such a noble air of the body, as it would be ridiculous to look for in any hired model of our academies.

Truth springs from the feelings of the heart. What shadow of it therefore can the modern artist hope for, by relying upon a vile model, whose soul is either too base to feel, or too stupid to express the passions, the sentiment his object claims? unhappy he! if experience and fancy fail him.

The beginning of many of *Plato's* dialogues, supposed to have been held in the Gymnasies, cannot raise our admiration of the generous souls of the Athenian youth, without giving us, at the same time, a strong presumption of a suitable nobleness in their outward carriage and bodily exercises.

The fairest youths danced undressed on the theatre; and *Sophocles,* the great *Sophocles,* when young, was the first who dared to entertain his fellow-citizens in this manner. *Phryne* went to bathe at the Eleusinian games, exposed to the eyes of all Greece, and rising from the water became the model of Venus Anadyomene. During certain solemnities the young Spartan maidens danced naked before the young men: strange this may seem, but will appear more probable, when we consider that the christians of the primitive church, both men and women, were dipped together in the same font.

Then every solemnity, every festival, afforded the artist opportunity to familiarize himself with all the beauties of Nature.

These frequent occasions of observing Nature, taught the Greeks to go on still farther. They began to form certain general ideas of beauty, with regard to the proportions of the inferiour parts, as well as of the whole frame: these they raised above the reach of mortality, according to the superiour model of some ideal nature.

Thus *Raphael* formed his Galatea, as we learn by his letter to Count Baltazar Castiglione, where he says, "Beauty being so seldom found among the fair, I avail myself of a certain ideal image."

According to those ideas, exalted above the pitch of material models, the Greeks formed their gods and heroes: the profile of the brow and nose of gods and goddesses is almost a straight line. The same they gave on their coins to queens, &c. but without indulging their fancy too much. Perhaps this profile was as peculiar to the ancient Greeks, as flat noses and little eyes to the Calmucks and Chinese; a supposition which receives some strength from the large eyes of all the heads on Greek coins and gems.

From the same ideas the Romans formed their Empresses on their coins. Livia and Agrippina have the profile of Artemisia and Cleopatra.

We observe, nevertheless, that the Greek artists in general, submitted to the law prescribed by the Thebans: "To do, under a penalty, their best in imitating Nature." For, where they could not possibly apply their easy profile, without endangering the resemblance, they followed Nature, as we see instanced in the beauteous head of Julia, the daughter of Titus, done by *Euodus.*

But to form a "just resemblance, and, at the same time, a handsomer one," being always the chief rule they observed, and which *Polygnotus* constantly went by; they must, of necessity, be supposed to have had in view a more beauteous and more perfect Nature. And when we are told, that some artists imitated *Praxiteles,* who took his concubine *Cratina* for the model of his Cnidian Venus; or that others formed the graces from *Lais;* it is to be understood that they did so, without neglecting these great laws of the art. Sensual beauty furnished the painter with all that nature could give; ideal beauty with the awful and sublime; from that he took the *Humane,* from this the *Divine.*

Let any one, sagacious enough to pierce into the depths of art, compare the whole system of the Greek figures with that of the moderns, by which, as they say, nature alone is imitated; good heaven! what a number of neglected beauties will he not discover!

For instance, in most of the modern figures, if the skin happens to be any where pressed, you see there several little smart wrinkles: when, on the contrary, the same parts, pressed in the same manner on Greek statues, by their soft undulations, form at last but one noble pressure. These masterpieces never show us the skin forcibly stretched, but softly embracing the firm flesh, which fills it up without any tumid expansion, and harmoniously follows its direction. There the skin never, as on modern bodies, appears in plaits distinct from the flesh.

Modern works are likewise distinguished from the ancient by parts; a crowd of small touches and dimples too sensibly drawn. In ancient works you find these distributed with sparing sagacity, and, as relative to a completer and more perfect Nature, offered but as hints, nay, often perceived only by the learned.

The probability still increases, that the bodies of the Greeks, as well as the works of their artists, were framed with more unity of system, a nobler harmony of parts, and a completeness of the whole, above our lean tensions and hollow wrinkles.

Such as would fain deny to the Greeks the advantages both of a more perfect Nature and of ideal Beauties, boast of the famous *Bernini,* as their great champion. He was of opinion, besides, that Nature was possessed of every requisite beauty: the only skill being to discover that. He boasted of having got rid of a prejudice concerning the Medicean Venus, whose charms he at first thought peculiar ones; but, after many careful researches, discovered them now and then in Nature.

He was taught then, by the Venus, to discover beauties in common Nature, which he had formerly thought peculiar to that statue, and but for it, never would have searched for them. Follows it not from thence, that the beauties of the Greek statues being discovered with less difficulty than those of Nature, are of course more affecting; not so diffused, but more harmoniously united? and if this be true, the pointing out of Nature as chiefly imitable, is leading us into a more tedious and bewildered road to the knowledge of perfect beauty, than setting up the ancients for that purpose: consequently *Bernini,* by adhering too strictly to Nature, acted against his own principles, as well as obstructed the progress of his disciples.

The imitation of beauty is either reduced to a single object, and is *individual,* or, gathering observations from single ones, *composes of these one whole.* The former we call copying, drawing a portrait; 'tis the straight way to Dutch forms and figures; whereas the other leads to general beauty, and its ideal images, and is the way the Greeks took. . . .

Their imitation discovering in the one every beauty diffused through Nature, showing in the other the pitch to which the most perfect Nature can elevate herself, when soaring above the senses, will quicken the genius of the artist, and shorten his discipleship: he will learn to think and draw with confidence, seeing here the fixed limits of human and divine beauty.

Building on this ground, his hand and senses directed by the Greek rule of beauty, the modern artist goes on the surest way to the imitation of Nature. The ideas of unity and perfection, which he acquired in meditating on antiquity, will help him to combine, and to ennoble the more scattered and weaker beauties of our Nature. Thus he will improve every beauty he discovers in it, and by comparing the beauties of nature with the ideal, form rules for himself.

Nothing would more decisively prove the advantages to be got by imitating the ancients, preferably to Nature, than an essay made with two youths of equal talents, by devoting the one to antiquity, the other to Nature: this would draw Nature as he finds her; if Italian, perhaps he might paint like *Caravaggio;* if Flemish, and lucky, like *Jac. Jordans;* if French, like *Stella:* the other would draw her as she directs, and paint like *Raphael.*

II. Contour

But even supposing that the imitation of Nature could supply all the artist wants, she never could bestow the precision of Contour, that characteristic distinction of the ancients.

The noblest Contour unites or circumscribes every part of the most perfect Nature, and the ideal beauties in the figures of the Greeks; or rather, contains them both. *Euphranor,* famous after the epoch of *Zeuxis,* is said to have first ennobled it.

Many of the moderns have attempted to imitate this Contour, but very few with success. The great *Rubens* is far from having attained either its precision or elegance, especially in the performances which he finished before he went to Italy, and studied the antiques.

The line by which Nature divides completeness from superfluity is but a small one, and, insensible as it often is, has been crossed even by the best moderns; while these, in shunning a meagre Contour, became corpulent, those, in shunning that, grew lean.

Among them all, only *Michael Angelo,* perhaps, may be said to have attained the antique; but only in strong muscular figures, heroic frames; not in those of tender youth; nor in female bodies, which, under his bold hand, grew Amazons.

The Greek artist, on the contrary, adjusted his Contour, in every figure, to the breadth of a single hair, even in the nicest and most tiresome performances, as gems. . . .

III. Drapery

By Drapery is to be understood all that the art teaches of covering the nudities, and folding the garments; and this is the third prerogative of the ancients.

The Greek Drapery, in order to help the Contour, was, for the most part, taken from thin and wet garments, which of course clasped the body, and discovered the shape. The robe of the Greek ladies was extremely thin; thence its epithet of Peplon.

In modern times the artists were forced to heap garments, and sometimes heavy ones, on each other, which of course could not fall into the flowing folds of the ancients. Hence the large-folded Drapery, by which the painter and sculptor may display as much skill as by the ancient manner. *Carlo Marat* and *Francis Solimena* may be called the chief masters of it: but the garments of the new Venetian school, by passing the bounds of nature and propriety, became stiff as brass.

IV. Expression

The last and most eminent characteristic of the Greek works is a noble simplicity and sedate grandeur in Gesture and Expression. As the bottom of the sea lies peaceful beneath a foaming surface, a great soul lies sedate beneath the strife of passions in Greek figures.

'Tis in the face of Laocoon this soul shines with full lustre, not confined however to the face, amidst the most violent sufferings. Pangs piercing every muscle, every labouring nerve; pangs which we almost feel ourselves, while we consider—not the face, nor the most expressive parts—

only the belly contracted by excruciating pains: these however, I say, exert not themselves with violence, either in the face or gesture. He pierces not heaven, like the Laocoon of *Virgil;* his mouth is rather opened to discharge an anxious overloaded groan, as *Sadolet* says; the struggling body and the supporting mind exert themselves with equal strength, nay balance all the frame.

Laocoon suffers, but suffers like the Philoctetes of *Sophocles:* we weeping feel his pains, but wish for the hero's strength to support his misery.

The Expression of so great a soul is beyond the force of mere nature. It was in his own mind the artist was to search for the strength of spirit with which he marked his marble. Greece enjoyed artists and philosophers in the same persons; and the wisdom of more than one Metrodorus directed art, and inspired its figures with more than common souls.

Had Laocoon been covered with a garb becoming an ancient sacrificer, his sufferings would have lost one half of their Expression. *Bernini* pretended to perceive the first effects of the operating venom in the numbness of one of the thighs.

Every action or gesture in Greek figures, not stamped with this character of sage dignity, but too violent, too passionate, was called "Parenthyrsos."

For, the more tranquillity reigns in a body, the fitter it is to draw the true character of the soul; which, in every excessive gesture, seems to rush from her proper centre, and being hurried away by extremes becomes unnatural. Wound up to the highest pitch of passion, she may force herself upon the duller eye; but the true sphere of her action is simplicity and calmness. In Laocoon sufferings alone had been Parenthyrsos; the artist therefore, in order to reconcile the significative and ennobling qualities of his soul, put him into a posture, allowing for the sufferings that were necessary, the next to a state of tranquillity: a tranquillity however that is characteristical: the soul will be herself—this individual—not the soul of mankind; sedate, but active; calm, but not indifferent or drowsy.

What a contrast! how diametrically opposite to this is the taste of our modern artists, especially the young ones! on nothing do they bestow their approbation, but contorsions and strange postures, inspired with boldness; this they pretend is done with spirit, with *Franchezza.* Contrast is the darling of their ideas; in it they fancy every perfection. They fill their performances with comet-like excentric souls, despising every thing but an Ajax or a Capaneus.

Arts have their infancy as well as men; they begin, as well as the artist, with froth and bombast. . . .

In all human actions flutter and rashness precede, sedateness and solidity follow: but time only can discover, and the judicious will admire these only: they are the characteristics of great masters; violent passions run away with their disciples.

This noble simplicity and sedate grandeur is also the true characteristic mark of the best and maturest Greek writings, of the epoch and school of *Socrates*. Possessed of these qualities *Raphael* became eminently great, and he owed them to the ancients.

That great soul of his, lodged in a beauteous body, was requisite for the first discovery of the true character of the ancients: he first felt all their beauties, and (what he was peculiarly happy in!) at an age when vulgar, unfeeling, and half-moulded souls overlook every higher beauty.

From *The History of Ancient Art* (1764)

After his arrival in Rome, in 1755, Winckelmann spent nine years in the intensive study of Egyptian, Etruscan, Greek, and Roman works which he found in the galleries, vaults, and gardens of Roman palaces, at Naples, and at the new excavations of Herculaneum. The result of his boundless diligence was the great History *which eclipsed all the antiquarian researches that had preceded it. Winckelmann's superiority rested on two main achievements. He was the first to put into systematic order the bewildering accumulation of sculptures, frescoes, decorative fragments, gems and coins, by bringing to bear on it not only his knowledge of literature, but also his powers of disciplined observation and critical comparison. More important still, he was able to gather the separate monuments and individual artists into one developmental sequence, the guiding principle of which was the progressive unfolding of style. This he saw as an irreversible and regular process, the typical main stages of which were most evident in the history of Greek art.*

At the center of his theory of art was the idea of beauty as a timeless, life-giving force, of which the evolving style merely presented temporal embodiments. Winckelmann's notion of beauty had little in common with the schemata of conventional art-philosophy. Though he theorized about unity and harmony, and acknowledged that beauty ultimately rested in God, his actual standard was concrete and natural: it was the human body, nude, and in the smoothness of adolescence. On it, he lavished his most enthusiastic praise and his finest descriptive passages. His idealism was a sublimated sensuousness. His language, even when employed in the expression of abstract ideas, is rich in images. He believed that "God had meant to make him a painter, and a great one at that," and it is clear that he had the gift of evoking visual form: his word-paintings of the Apollo of Belvedere, the Torso, and the Niobids contributed to the formation of the neoclassical style in art.[4]

On Beauty

Beauty, as the loftiest mark and the central point of art, demands some preliminary discussion, in which I should wish to satisfy both myself and the reader; but this is a wish of difficult gratification in either respect.

For beauty is one of the great mysteries of nature, whose influence we all see and feel; but a general, distinct idea of its essential must be classed among the truths yet undiscovered. If this idea were geometrically clear, men would not differ in their opinions upon the beautiful, and it would be easy to prove what true beauty is; still less could there be one class of men of so unfortunate sensibility, and another of so perverse self-conceit, that the former would create for themselves a false beauty, and the latter refuse to receive a correct idea of true beauty.

Why Opinions on Beauty Differ

This difference of opinion is shown still more strongly in the judgment passed upon the beauties impersonated by art, than upon those in nature itself. The cause lies in our passions, which with most men are excited by the first look, and the senses are already gratified, when reason, unsatisfied, is seeking to discover and enjoy the charm of true beauty. It is not, then, beauty which captivates us, but sensuality. Consequently, young persons, in whom the passions are in a state of excitement and ferment, will look upon those faces as divine, which, though not strictly beautiful, have the charm of tender and passionate expression; and they will be less affected by a truly beautiful woman, even with the shape and majesty of Juno, whose gestures and actions evince modesty and decorum.

The ideas of beauty with most artists are formed from their first crude impressions, which are seldom weakened or destroyed by loftier beauties, especially when they cannot improve their minds by recurring to the beauties of the ancients.

In others, the climate has not allowed the gentle feeling of pure beauty to mature; it has either been confirmed in them by art,—that is, by constantly and studiously employing their scientific knowledge in the

---

[4] The translation used is that of G. Henry Lodge, *The History of Ancient Art*, Boston, 1880. The particular sections quoted are "On Beauty," I, 302; "Opinions on Beauty," I, 304; "Color," I, 308; "Unity," I, 310; "Generality," I, 311; "The Shape of Beauty," I, 311; "The Torso," II, 263; "Apollo," II, 312.

representation of youthful beauties—as in Michael Angelo, or become in time utterly corrupted, as was the case with Bernini by a vulgar flattery of the coarse and uncultivated, in attempting to render everything more intelligible to them. The former busied himself in the contemplation of lofty beauty; this is evident from his poems, some of which have been published; in them his thoughts relative to it are expressed in elevated language, worthy of the subject. In powerful figures he is wonderful; but, from the cause before mentioned, his female and youthful figures are in shape, action, and gesture, creatures of another world. The very course which led Michael Angelo to impassable places and steep cliffs plunged Bernini, on the contrary, into bogs and pools; for he sought to dignify, as it were, by exaggeration, forms of the most ordinary. His figures are those of vulgar people who have suddenly met with good fortune, and their expression is oftentimes opposed to the action, as when Hannibal laughed in the extremity of his grief. Yet this artist long held undisputed sway, and homage is paid to him even now.

But we ourselves differ as to beauty—probably more than we do even in taste and smell—whenever our ideas respecting it are deficient in clearness. It will not be easy to find a hundred men who would agree as to all the points of beauty in any one face—I speak of those who have not thought profoundly on the subject. The handsomest man that I have seen in Italy was not the handsomest in the eyes of all, not even of those who prided themselves on being observant of the beauty of our sex. . . .

Color

Color assists beauty; generally, it heightens beauty and its forms, but it does not constitute it; just as the taste of wine is more agreeable, from its color, when drunk from a transparent glass, than from the most costly golden cup. Color, however, should have but little share in our consideration of beauty, because the essence of beauty consists, not in color, but in shape, and on this point enlightened minds will at once agree. As white is the color which reflects the greatest number of rays of light, and consequently is the most easily perceived, a beautiful body will, accordingly, be the more beautiful the whiter it is, just as we see that all figures in gypsum, when freshly formed, strike us as larger than the statues from which they are made. A Negro might be called handsome, when the conformation of his face is handsome. A traveller assures us that daily association with Negroes diminishes the disagreeableness of their color, and displays what is beautiful in them; just as the color of bronze and of the black and greenish basalt does not detract from the beauty of the antique heads.

Unity

The highest beauty is in God; and our idea of human beauty advances towards perfection in proportion as it can be imagined in conformity and harmony with that highest Existence which, in our conception of unity and indivisibility, we distinguish from matter. This idea of beauty is like an essence extracted from matter by fire; it seeks to beget unto itself a creature formed after the likeness of the first rational being designed in the mind of the Divinity. The forms of such a figure are simple and flowing, and various in their unity; and for this reason they are harmonious, just as a sweet and pleasing tone can be extracted from bodies the parts of which are uniform. All beauty is heightened by unity and simplicity, as is everything which we do and say; for whatever is great in itself is elevated, when executed and uttered with simplicity. It is not more strictly circumscribed, nor does it lose any of its greatness, because the mind can survey and measure it with a glance, and comprehend and embrace it in a single idea; but the very readiness with which it may be embraced places it before us in its true greatness, and the mind is enlarged, and likewise elevated, by the comprehension of it. Everything which we must consider in separate pieces, or which we cannot survey at once, from the number of its constituent parts, loses thereby some portion of its greatness, just as a long road is shortened by many objects presenting themselves on it, or by many inns at which a stop can be made. The harmony which ravishes the soul does not consist in arpeggios, and tied and slurred notes, but in simple, long-drawn tones. This is the reason why a large palace appears small, when it is overloaded with ornament, and a house large, when elegant and simple in its style.

Generality

From unity proceeds another attribute of lofty beauty, the absence of individuality; that is, the forms of it are described neither by points nor lines other than those which shape beauty merely, and consequently produce a figure which is neither peculiar to any particular individual, nor yet expresses any one state of the mind or affection of the passions, because these blend with it strange lines, and mar the unity. According to this idea, beauty should be like the best kind of water, drawn from the spring itself; the less taste it has, the more healthful it is considered, because free from all foreign admixture.

Since, however, there is no middle state in human nature between pain and pleasure, and the passions are the winds which impel our bark over the sea of life, pure beauty alone cannot be the sole object of our consideration; we must place it also in a state of action and of passion, which we comprehend in art under the term *Expression*.

The Shape of Beauty

The shape of beauty is either *individual*—that is, confined to an imitation of one individual—or it is a selection of beautiful parts from many individuals, and their union into one, which we call *ideal*.

The conformation of beauty commenced with individual beauty, with an imitation of a beautiful male form, even in the representation of the gods; and, in the blooming days of sculpture, the statues of goddesses were actually made after the likeness of beautiful women, even of those whose favors were venal.

Among beautiful youths, artists found the cause of beauty in unity, variety, and harmony. For the forms of a beautiful body are determined by lines the centre of which is constantly changing, and which, if continued, would never describe circles. They are, consequently, more simple, but also more complex, than a circle, which, however large or small it may be, always has the same centre, and either includes others, or is included in others. This diversity was sought after by the Greeks in works of all kinds; and their discernment of its beauty led them to introduce the same system even into the form of their utensils and vases, whose easy and elegant outline is drawn after the same rule, that is, by a line which must be found by means of several circles, for all these works have an elliptical figure, and herein consists their beauty. The greater unity there is in the junction of the forms, and in the flowing of one out of another, so much the greater is the beauty of the whole.

From this great unity of youthful forms, their limits flow imperceptibly one into another, and the precise point of height of many, and the line which bounds them, cannot be accurately determined. This is the reason why the delineation of a youthful body, in which everything is and is yet to come, appears and yet does not appear, is more difficult than that of an adult or aged figure. In the former of these two, the adult, nature has completed, and consequently determined, her work of formation; in the latter, she begins again to destroy the structure; in both, therefore, the junction of the parts is clearly visible. To deviate from the outline in bodies having strongly developed muscles, or to strengthen or exaggerate the prominence of muscles or other parts, is not so great an error as the slightest deviation in youthful figures.

But nature and the structure of the most beautiful bodies are rarely without fault. They have forms which can either be found more perfect in other bodies, or which may be imagined more perfect. In conformity to this teaching of experience, those wise artists, the ancients, acted as a skillful gardener does, who ingrafts different shoots of excellent sorts upon the same stock; and, as a bee gathers from many flowers, so were their ideas of beauty not limited to the beautiful in a single individual, but they sought to unite the beautiful parts of many beautiful bodies. They purified their images from all personal feelings, by which the mind is diverted from the truly beautiful.

The Apollo of Belvedere

Among all the works of antiquity which have escaped destruction the statue of Apollo is the highest ideal of art. The artist has constructed this work entirely on the ideal, and has employed in its structure just so much only of the material as was necessary to carry out his design and render it visible. This Apollo exceeds all other figures of him as much as the Apollo of Homer excels him whom later poets paint. His stature is loftier than that of man, and his attitude speaks of the greatness with which he is filled. An eternal spring, as in the happy fields of Elysium, clothes with the charms of youth the graceful manliness of ripened years, and plays with softness and tenderness about the proud shape of his limbs. Let thy spirit penetrate into the kingdom of incorporeal beauties, and strive to become a creator of a heavenly nature, in order that thy mind may be filled with beauties that are elevated above nature; for there is nothing mortal here, nothing which human necessities require. Neither blood-vessels nor sinews heat and stir this body, but a heavenly essence, diffusing itself like a gentle stream, seems to fill the whole contour of the figure. He has pursued the Python, against which he uses his bow for the first time; with vigorous step he has overtaken the monster and slain it. His lofty look, filled with a consciousness of power, seems to rise far above his victory, and to gaze into infinity. Scorn sits upon his lips, and his nostrils are swelling with suppressed anger, which mounts even to the proud forehead; but the peace which floats upon it in blissful calm remains undisturbed, and his eye is full of sweetness as when the Muses gathered around him seeking to embrace him. The Father of the gods in all the images of him which we have remaining, and which art venerates, does not approach so nearly the grandeur in which he manifested himself to the understanding of the divine poet, as he does here in the countenance of his son, and the individual beauties of the other deities are here as in the person of Pandora assembled together, a forehead of Jupiter, pregnant with the Goddess of Wisdom, and eyebrows the contractions of which express their will, the grandly arched eyes of the queen of the gods, and a mouth shaped like that whose touch stirred with delight the loved Branchus. The soft hair plays about the divine head as if agitated by a gentle breeze, like the slender waving tendrils of the noble vine; it seems to be anointed with the oil of the gods, and tied by the Graces with pleasing display on the crown of his head. In the presence of this miracle of art I forget all else, and I myself take a lofty position for the purpose of looking upon it in a worthy manner. My breast seems to enlarge and swell with reverence, like the breasts of those who were filled with the spirit of prophecy, and I feel myself transported to Delos and into the Lycæan groves—places which Apollo honored by his presence—for my image seems to receive life and motion, like the beautiful creation of Pygmalion. How is it possible to paint and describe it! Art itself must counsel me, and guide my hand in filling up hereafter the first outlines which I here have sketched. As they who were unable to reach the heads of the divinities which they wished to crown deposited the garlands at the feet of them, so I place at the feet of this image the conception which I have presented of it.

The Torso

In this period, I believe, must be placed Apollonius, son of Nestor of Athens, and master of the so-called Torso in the Belvedere, that is, of the stump of a reposing and deified Hercules.

Abused and mutilated to the utmost, and without head, arms, or legs, as this statue is, it shows itself even now to those who have the power to look deeply into the secrets of art with all the splendor of its former beauty. The artist has presented in this Hercules a lofty ideal of a body elevated above nature, and a shape at the full development of manhood, such as it might be if exalted to the degree of divine sufficiency. He appears here purified from the dross of humanity, and after having attained immortality and a seat among the gods; for he is represented without need of human nourishment, or further use of his powers. No veins are visible, and the belly is made only to enjoy, not to receive, and to be full without being filled. The right arm was placed over the head, as we are able to determine from the position of the fragment which remains, for the purpose of representing him in repose after all his toils—this attitude indicating repose.

In this position, with the head turned upwards, his face probably had a pleased expression as he meditated with satisfaction on the great deeds which he had achieved; this feeling even the back seems to indicate, which is bent, as if the hero was absorbed in lofty reflections. In that powerfully developed chest we behold in imagination the breast against which the giant Geryon was squeezed and in the length and strength of the thigh we recognize the unwearied hero who pursued and overtook the brazen-footed stag, and travelled through countless lands even to the very confines of the world.

The artist may admire in the outlines of this body the perpetual flowing of one form into another, and the undulating lines which rise and fall like waves, and become swallowed up in one another. He will find that no copyist can be sure of correctness, since the undulating movement which he thinks he is following turns imperceptibly away, and leads both the hand and eye astray by taking another direction. The bones appear covered with a fatty skin, the muscles are full without superfluity, and no other statue can be found which shows so well balanced a plumpness; we might indeed say that this Hercules seems to be the production of an earlier period of art even more than the Apollo.

Gotthold Ephraim Lessing (1729–1781)

A dramatic author of high rank, comparable to Diderot in his choice of modern, middle-class themes, Lessing brought to the criticism of art insights which he had gained in his own literary practice. The immediate stimulus for his essay on Laocoon *came from the passage in Winckelmann's* Thoughts on the Imitation of Greek Works, *which he quotes at the outset. But his main purpose was not to refute Winckelmann, with whom he agreed on most essentials; he meant, rather, to disentangle the confusion of literary and pictorial values which generations of theorists had perpetrated under the slogan of "ut pictura poesis." This confusion had misled some artists into painted literature or stale allegory, and it had betrayed many critics into nonsense. It had caused Winckelmann to compare the marble group in the Vatican with some lines in Virgil's* Aeneid, *and to draw from this comparison, a conclusion about the style and quality of Greek sculpture. Lessing not only demonstrated the falsity of the comparison and of the conclusion; he also proved that the difference between the Greek sculpture and the Latin poem was rooted in their fundamental formal dimensions, in space and time, rather than their particular stylistic character. His analysis went deeper than that of other critics, and touched on the reality of the psychological experience of mass and motion, duration and sequence which defines the different modes of artistic expression.*

But Lessing himself was not free from literary preconceptions about art. He took for granted, as did Winckelmann, that the Laocoon *exemplified the "noble simplicity and quiet greatness" of high classical Greek art, while it actually resembles, in its melodramatic animation, the Baroque style which Lessing, no less than Winckelmann, held in contempt. What he had read about Laocoon's greatness of soul imposed itself on his vision as he studied engravings of the tangled group, and veiled for him the work's unclassical character.[5]*

[5] Translated by Ellen Frothingham, *Laocoon, An Essay Upon the Limits of Painting and Poetry*, New York, The Noonday Press, 1957.

From *Laocoon, On the Limitations of Painting and Poetry* (1766)

I.

The chief and universal characteristic of the Greek masterpieces in painting and sculpture consists, according to Winckelmann, in a noble simplicity and quiet grandeur, both of attitude and expression. [Lessing's reference is to Winckelmann's description of the Laocoon, quoted on p. 11.] . . .

The remark which lies at the root of this criticism—that suffering is not expressed in the countenance of Laocoon with the intensity which its violence would lead us to expect—is perfectly just. That this very point, where a shallow observer would judge the artist to have fallen short of nature and not to have attained the true pathos of suffering, furnishes the clearest proof of his wisdom, is also unquestionable. But in the reason which Winckelmann assigns for this wisdom, and the universality of the rule which he deduces from it, I venture to differ from him. . . .

A cry is the natural expression of bodily pain. Homer's wounded heroes not infrequently fall with a cry to the ground. Venus screams aloud at a scratch, not as being the tender goddess of love, but because suffering nature will have its rights. Even the iron Mars, on feeling the lance of Diomedes, bellows as frightfully as if ten thousand raging warriors were roaring at once, and fills both armies with terror.

High as Homer exalts his heroes in other respects above human nature, they yet remain true to it in their sensitiveness to pain and injuries and in the expression of their feelings by cries or tears or revilings. Judged by their deeds they are creatures of a higher order; in their feelings they are genuine human beings. . . .

I come now to my conclusion. If it be true that a cry, as an expression of bodily pain, is not inconsistent with nobility of soul, especially according to the views of the ancient Greeks, then the desire to represent such a soul cannot be the reason why the artist has refused to imitate this cry in his marble. He must have had some other reason for deviating in this respect from his rival, the poet, who expresses it with deliberate intention.

II.

. . . The Greek artist represented nothing that was not beautiful. "Who would want to paint you when no one wants to look at you?" says an old epigrammatist to a misshapen man. Many a modern artist would say, "No matter how misshapen you are, I will paint you. Though people may not like to look at you, they will be glad to look at my picture; not as a portrait of you, but as a proof of my skill in making so close a copy of such a monster."

The fondness for making a display with mere manual dexterity, ennobled by no worth in the subject, is too natural not to have produced among the Greeks a Pauson and a Pyreicus. They had such painters, but meted out to them strict justice. Pauson, who confined himself to the beauties of ordinary nature, and whose depraved taste liked best to represent the imperfections and deformities of humanity, lived in the most abandoned poverty; and Pyreicus, who painted barbers' rooms, dirty workshops, donkeys, and kitchen herbs, with all the diligence of a Dutch painter, as if such things were rare or attractive in nature, acquired the surname of Rhyparographer, the dirt-painter. The rich voluptuaries, indeed, paid for his works their weight in gold as if by this fictitious valuation to atone for their insignificance.

Even the magistrates considered this subject a matter worthy their attention, and confined the artist by force within his proper sphere. The law of the Thebans commanding him to make his copies more beautiful than the originals, and never under pain of punishment less so, is well known. This was no law against bunglers, as has been supposed by critics generally, and even by Junius himself, but was aimed against the Greek Ghezzi, and condemned the unworthy artifice of obtaining a likeness by exaggerating the deformities of the model. It was, in fact, a law against caricature.

We laugh when we read that the very arts among the ancients were subject to the control of civil law; but we have no right to laugh. Laws should unquestionably usurp no sway over science, for the object of science is truth. Truth is a necessity of the soul, and to put any restraint upon the gratification of this essential want is tyranny. The object of art, on the contrary, is pleasure, and pleasure is not indispensable. What kind and what degree of pleasure shall be permitted may justly depend on the law-giver.

The plastic arts especially, besides the inevitable influence which they exercise on the character of a nation, have power to work one effect which demands the careful attention of the law. Beautiful statues fashioned from beautiful men reacted upon their creators, and the state was indebted for its beautiful men to beautiful statues. With us the susceptible imagination of the mother seems to express itself only in monsters. . . .

There are passions and degrees of passion whose expression produces the most hideous contortions of the face, and throws the whole body into such unnatural positions as to destroy all the beautiful lines that mark it when in a state of greater repose. These passions the old artists either refrained altogether from representing, or softened into emotions which were capable of being expressed with some degree of beauty.

Anguish was softened into sadness. Where that was impossible, and where the representation of intense grief would belittle as well as disfigure, how did Timanthes manage? There is a well-known picture by him of the sacrifice of Iphigenia, wherein he gives to the countenance of every spectator a fitting degree of sadness, but veils the face of the father, on which should have been depicted the most intense suffering.

Apply this to the Laocoon and we have the cause we were seeking. The master was striving to attain the greatest beauty under the given conditions of bodily pain. Pain, in its disfiguring extreme, was not compatible with beauty, and must therefore be softened. Screams must be reduced to sighs, not because screams would betray weakness, but because they would deform the countenance to a repulsive degree. Imagine Laocoon's mouth open, and judge. Let him scream, and see. It was, before, a figure to inspire compassion in its beauty and suffering. Now it is ugly, abhorrent, and we gladly avert our eyes from a painful spectacle, destitute of the beauty which alone could turn our pain into the sweet feeling of pity for the suffering object.

The simple opening of the mouth, apart from the violent and repulsive contortion it causes in other parts of the face, is a blot on a painting and a cavity in a statue productive of the worst possible effect.

III.

But, as already observed, the realm of art has in modern times been greatly enlarged. Its imitations are allowed to extend over all visible nature, of which beauty constitutes but a small part. Truth and expression are taken as its first law. As nature always sacrifices beauty to higher ends, so should the artist subordinate it to his general purpose, and not pursue it further than truth and expression allow. Enough that truth and expression convert what is unsightly in nature into a beauty of art.

Allowing this idea to pass unchallenged at present for whatever it is worth, are there not other independent considerations which should set bounds to expression, and prevent the artist from choosing for his imitation the culminating point of any action?

The single moment of time to which art must confine itself, will lead us, I think, to such considerations. Since the artist can use but a single moment of ever-changing nature, and the painter must further confine his study of this one moment to a single point of view, while their works are made not simply to be looked at, but to be contemplated long and often, evidently the most fruitful moment and the most fruitful aspect of that moment must be chosen. Now that only is fruitful which allows free play to the imagination. The more we see the more we must be able to imagine; and the more we imagine, the more we must think we see. But no moment in the whole course of an action is so disadvantageous in this respect as that of its culmination. There is nothing beyond, and to present the uttermost to the eye is to bind the wings of Fancy, and compel her, since she cannot soar beyond the impression made on the senses, to employ herself with feebler images, shunning as her limit the visible fullness already expressed. When, for instance, Laocoon sighs, imagination can hear him cry; but if he cry, imagination can neither mount a step higher, nor fall a step lower, without seeing him in a more endurable, and therefore less interesting, condition. We hear him merely groaning, or we see him already dead.

Again, since this single moment receives from art an unchanging duration, it should express nothing essentially transitory. All phenomena, whose nature it is suddenly to break out and as suddenly to disappear, which can remain as they are but for a moment; all such phenomena, whether agreeable or otherwise, acquire through the perpetuity conferred upon them by art such an unnatural appearance, that the impression they produce becomes weaker with every fresh observation, till the whole subject at last wearies or disgusts us. . . . Pain which is so violent as to extort a scream, either soon abates or it must destroy the sufferer. Again, if a man of firmness and endurance cry, he does not do so unceasingly, and only this apparent continuity in art makes the cry degenerate into womanish weakness or childish impatience. This, at least, the sculptor of the Laocoon had to guard against, even had a cry not been an offence against beauty, and were suffering without beauty a legitimate subject of art. . . .

IV.

A review of the reasons here alleged for the moderation observed by the sculptor of the Laocoon in the expression of bodily pain, shows them to lie wholly in the peculiar object of his art and its necessary limitations. Scarce one of them would be applicable to poetry.

When Virgil's Laocoon screams, who stops to think that a scream necessitates an open mouth, and that an open mouth is ugly? Enough that "clamores horrendos ad sidera tollit" is fine to the ear, no matter what its effect on the eye. Whoever requires a beautiful picture has missed the whole intention of the poet.

Further, nothing obliges the poet to concentrate his picture into a single moment. He can take up every action, if he will, from its origin, and carry it through all possible changes to its issue. Every change, which would require from the painter a separate picture, costs him but a single touch; a touch, perhaps, which, taken by itself, might offend the imagination, but which, anticipated, as it has been, by what preceded, and softened and atoned for by what follows, loses its individual effect in the admirable result of the whole. . . .

Who blames the poet, then? Rather must we acknowledge that he was right in introducing the cry, as the sculptor was in omitting it. . . . In art the difficulty appears to lie more in the execution than in the invention, while with poetry the contrary is the case. There the execution seems easy in comparison with the invention. Had Virgil copied the twining of the serpents about Laocoon and his sons from the marble, then his description would lose its chief merit; for what we consider the more difficult part had been done for him. The first conception of this grouping in the imagination is a far greater achievement than the expression of it in words. But if the sculptor have borrowed the grouping from the poet, we still consider him deserving of great praise, although he have not the merit of the first conception. For to give expression in marble is incalculably more difficult than to give it in words. We weigh invention and execution in opposite scales, and are inclined to require from the master as much less of one as he has given us more of the other.

There are even cases where the artist deserves more credit for copying Nature through the medium of the poet's imitation than directly from herself. The painter who makes a beautiful landscape from the description of a Thomson, does more than one who takes his picture at first hand from nature. The latter sees his model before him; the former must, by an effort of imagination, think he sees it. One makes a beautiful picture from vivid, sensible impressions, the other from the feeble, uncertain representations of arbitrary signs.

From this natural readiness to excuse the artist from the merit of invention, has arisen on his part an equally natural indifference to it. Perceiving that invention could never be his strong point, but that his fame must rest chiefly on execution, he ceased to care whether his theme were new or old, whether it had been used once or a hundred times, belonged to himself or another. He kept within the narrow range of a few subjects, grown familiar to himself and the public, and directed all his invention to the introducing of some change in the treatment, some new combination of the old objects. . . . Considering now these two points: first, that invention and novelty in the subject are by no means what we chiefly require from the painter; and secondly, that a familiar subject helps and quickens the effect of his art, I think we . . . may even be inclined to praise as a wise and, as far as we are concerned, a beneficent forbearance on the part of the artist, what seemed to us at first a deficiency in art and a curtailment of our enjoyment. If it be true that painting employs wholly different signs or means of imitation from poetry—the one using forms and colors in space, the other articulate sounds in time— and if signs must unquestionably stand in convenient relation with the thing signified, then signs arranged side by side can represent only objects existing side by side, or whose parts so exist, while consecutive signs can express only objects which succeed each other, or whose parts succeed each other, in time.

Objects which exist side by side, or whose parts so exist, are called bodies. Consequently bodies with their visible properties are the peculiar subjects of painting.

Objects which succeed each other, or whose parts succeed each other in time, are actions. Consequently actions are the peculiar subjects of poetry.

All bodies, however, exist not only in space, but also in time. They continue, and, at any moment of their continuance, may assume a different appearance and stand in different relations. Every one of these momentary appearances and groupings was the result of a preceding, may become the cause of a following, and is therefore the centre of a present, action. Consequently painting can imitate actions also, but only as they are suggested through forms.

Actions, on the other hand, cannot exist independently, but must always be joined to certain agents. In so far as those agents are bodies or are regarded as such, poetry describes also bodies, but only indirectly through actions.

Painting, in its coexistent compositions, can use but a single moment of an action, and must therefore choose the most pregnant one, the one most suggestive of what has gone before and what is to follow.

Poetry, in its progressive imitations, can use but a single attribute of bodies, and must choose that one which gives the most vivid picture of the body as exercised in this particular action.

Giovanni Battista Piranesi (1720–1778)

Among the antiquarians whose researches gave momentum to the classical revival, Piranesi occupied a peculiar position. He was a printmaker of powerful originality, whose views of Roman ruins, no less than his own architectural fantasies, carry a sense of mystery and menace quite unlike the pallor of most classicist work. In his intensity, he resembled Winckelmann, that other eccentric, though he sharply disagreed with Winckelmann's praise of Greek over Roman art. Rather than by any beauty or harmony of form, Piranesi was moved by the hard grandeur and boldness of Roman work. Horace Walpole wrote of Piranesi in 1771:

"*This delicate redundance of ornament growing into our architecture might perhaps be checked, if our artists would study the sublime dreams of Piranesi, who seems to have conceived visions of Rome beyond what it boasted even in the meridian of its splendor. Savage as Salvator Rosa, fierce as Michael Angelo, and exuberant as Rubens, he has imagined scenes that would startle geometry, and exhaust the Indies to realize. He piles palaces on bridges, and temples on palaces, and scales heaven with mountains of edifices. Yet what taste in his boldness! what grandeur in his wildness! what labour and thought both in his rashness and details! Architecture, indeed, has in a manner two sexes: its masculine dignity can only exert its muscle in public works and at public expense; its softer beauties come better within the compass of private residence and enjoyment.*" [6] *Piranesi's publication of plates of Roman ruins, entitled* **Magnificenza ed Architettura de' Romani** *(1761–1762), reflected his intensive archaeological and topographical studies and at the same time pursued a polemical aim, stated in the Preface from which the following excerpts are taken. It was Piranesi's intention to defend the claim of Roman architecture to high excellence and originality against those scholars who, like Winckelmann, looked on Roman art as essentially imitative of and inferior to the Greek. His line of argument strangely combines Enlightenment rationality—the high value placed on the utility of engineering work —and an irrational enthusiasm for the sheer grandeur of Roman works and the dignity of national past.* [7]

From *Magnificenza ed Architettura de' Romani* (1761–1762)

I certainly should never have imagined that the Romans might some day be accused of being small-minded and crude. The majority of their works, to be sure, have been destroyed by the ravages of time and war, but whenever I see their magnificent monuments in Rome and throughout Italy, I am astonished that such a judgment should have occurred to men possessing any instruction at all. Yet people who attribute everything to the Greeks do hold this opinion of the Romans, and since this opinion is spreading more and more among foreign nations, I deem it to be fitting for one of my profession to examine the whole matter more thoroughly, so that, when all the arguments have been weighed, it will become easier for the fair-minded to decide what judgment he should make.

. . . The Etruscan nation, because of its antiquity and wealth, had the time and leisure to bring all the arts to their highest perfection. As to its antiquity, Dionysius, citing the various opinions of ancient writers who

[6] From the "Advertisement" of Horace Walpole's *Anecdotes of Painting*, 4th edition, London, 1786, IV, 398.

[7] G. B. Piranesi, *Della Magnificenza ed Architettura de' Romani*, ed. Firmin-Didot, Paris, 1836, pp. 4 ff.

had written about the origins of the Etruscans before him, supports those who regarded them as indigenous to Italy: "Clearly, this nation is very ancient and evidently had nothing in common with other nations, either in customs or in language."

. . . From sources such as these, the other arts and, together with them, the proper way of building came to Rome, since it is usual that men try to imitate the best of others, as soon as they have the time. The Romans, seeing the admirable edifices of the Etruscans . . . could not help but be delighted with what they had seen, and wanted to have this kind of building in Rome for themselves, now that they had grown in importance and achieved a greater reputation than any of their neighbors. In the year CCLX, they therefore established the magistracy of the *Ediles* whose first responsibility it was to care for the public buildings. Anyone who has read Roman history knows how rapidly the number of these buildings increased from the very beginning, and particularly the temples of the gods which the Romans built, motivated either by their own superstitions or by some vow uttered in time of great danger. I am certain that, had these buildings been mere hovels or modest huts, the Romans would not have created an illustrious magistrate to preside over this work. I will admit that the majority of Rome's citizens did not have magnificent dwellings in those early times. They sacrificed their private means for the good of the Republic, but when there was a question of erecting or repairing public works and temples, they would disregard expense and not allow anything to be done which might be criticized as being unworthy of the Roman people and the honor of the gods.

. . . After considering these matters which show clearly that the Romans had enough art to provide for utility and public embellishments, I shall turn to other, even more remarkable works. The first of these will be the *Cloaca Maxima,* which allows us to remark that even where there seemed to be little need for magnificence, as in this structure which was hidden from view, the Romans chose nonetheless to display magnificence all the more. . . . Dionysius writes of Priscus: "Tarquinius Priscus also undertook the excavation of the sewers which are underground canals that carry to the Tiber all the waters from the streets. One can hardly express how marvellous these works are. I certainly count among the three most magnificent works of Rome, among those which particularly show the grandeur of her Empire, the aqueducts, the paved roads, and the sewers, bearing in mind not only their usefulness but also their cost. . . ."

. . . The other truly wonderful work which enhances the magnificence of Rome is the system of aqueducts. From Frontinus we learn that, of the nine main streams which in ancient times flowed into Rome, three had already been artificially channelled before Rome subjugated Greece, namely the Appia, the old Anione, and the Marcia.

These three conduits, taken together, comprise 110 miles of underground river and about 16 miles of construction above ground which consist partly of foundations, partly of arches. The ruins of some of these conduits in Rome proper and in the environs of Rome show that both the substructures and the arches were made in part of stone, in part of brick, and that the subterranean channels were made large enough for the workmen to move about easily. . . .

. . . There remains the third class of work which Dionysius used as an argument for the grandeur of the Roman Empire, namely the paved roads.

Considering only these three kinds of monuments, we might reflect on the question of whether they could have been undertaken by men who were crude and had no feeling for art. Seeing that all these works required men of the greatest talent and deeply conversant with architecture, we might further investigate whether the Romans used Greek art in achieving these works. Before coming to any decision, we ought to listen to what Strabo has to say: "While it appears that the Greeks reached the highest level in building cities, because of their concern for beauty, for fortifications, harbors, and the general welfare of the country, the Romans strove, on the other hand, to do the things which the Greeks had neglected, namely the paving of highways, the channelling of streams, and the construction of underground sewers to carry the city's refuse into the Tiber. They paved the roads in the countryside, razing the hills and levelling the valleys, so that ship cargoes could be transported overland in carts; and they built sewers with stone vaults which are wide enough in some places to let through a cart loaded with hay."

. . . Leaving aside the loftier sciences: where, if not in Italy did Latin poetry arise, for which reason Petrarch was crowned in Rome? Where were sculpture and painting reborn, if not in the work of Giotto, Michelangelo, and Raphael who not only revived them but brought them to perfection? Finally, where was Greek architecture revived, buried as it had been in the ruins and hidden in the codices, if not in the work of Bramante, Baldassare da Siena, the same Michelangelo, Palladio, and those many others who brought it back to the open light? . . ."

ACADEMY

Academies of art, regardless of whether or not they are capable of producing artists, can be effective instruments for the central control of education and patronage. Originally established for this purpose, in an age of absolutism, they acquired new importance under the more liberal auspices of enlightened monarchy, as self-governing, professional bodies, empowered to legislate in the arts and to mediate between the demands of society and the interest of artists. The advent of Neoclassicism, itself a product of the Enlightenment, gave a further stimulus to the development of academies, since the scholarly and theoretical bent of this movement deeply suited the academic preference for the intellectual over the technical or craftsmanlike approach to art. The number of academic foundations increased sharply; in 1740, Europe had fewer than 40, in 1790 it had more than 100 academies.

The official character of the academy, its claim to authority and desire for stability were bound to make it conservative. Academic doctrine rested ultimately on principles not open to debate. The range of academic thought therefore was narrow, and remained confined to a small repertory of ideas to which the Enlightenment contributed little that was new or substantial. The limitation and fixity of academic doctrine accounts for its remarkable coherence, but it also makes clear why it had to come into conflict with the more dynamic thought of the period. Doctrinal confinement led academies to adopt the peculiar style of teaching which came to be their trademark. It made them deal with reality, both in nature and in art, as if it were composed of static quantities which could be taken apart, judged separately, and recombined at will; it misled them into mechanical routine, tight specialization, and imitative eclecticism.

Anton Raphael Mengs (1728–1778)

Mengs' father, a court painter at Dresden, dedicated his infant son to art, and mercilessly whipped the boy into precocious virtuosity. Mengs rose to be a European celebrity, a thoroughly cosmopolitan artist whose fame outshone that of the two geniuses whose careers crossed his own— Tiepolo and Goya. The Parnassus *ceiling in the Villa Albani (1761), masterpiece of his Roman period, was a manifesto of Neoclassicism and a challenge to the dying Rococo; Winckelmann believed that Raphael would have bowed before it. And it was at the suggestion of Winckelmann, as whose mentor and artistic advisor Mengs had acted in Rome, that he published his* Thoughts on Beauty and Taste in Painting *(1762). Dry, and rather poorly written, this treatise was nevertheless an influential instrument of academic teaching in its time. It rests on a theory of beauty, the elements of which are derived from Bellori and the French Academy. The wisdom of the ancients, according to Mengs, had extracted the idea of beauty from nature and given it a nearly perfect visible form in art. The great masters of the Renaissance rediscovered partial aspects of beauty and embodied them in their less perfect works. Modern artists can do no better than to search for beauty in earlier art, gathering its various parts from different sources, as the bee gathers honey from many flowers, and make it their own by a judicious choice and blending of borrowed elements. Salomon Gessner wrote appreciatively:*

How priceless is Mengs' little book! It contains more food for thought on art than many a heavy tome. Though as a philosopher he is not always clear, when he speaks as an artist he expresses himself with as much force, lucidity, purity of taste, and fine philosophical observation as one could wish for from a contemporary artist.

From *Thoughts on Beauty and Taste in Painting* (1762)

The History of Taste [8]

When order finally returned to the world, the arts, too, reemerged from the void. In the beginning, the descendants of the oppressed Greeks brought painting back to Italy, but their knowledge of this art was limited to the use of pictures in Catholic worship, and it was so imperfect as to show merely their good will: they were too poor and too despised to raise the art. But when painting became popular among the Italians, who were then rich and happy, art was raised a little from darkness by certain men, most of all by Giotto. Discrimination, however, comes only with knowledge. All artists who preceded Raphael, Titian, and Correggio sought only pure imitation, hence there was no taste at all in this period. A painting was like chaos. Some painters wanted to imitate nature, but could not; others could imitate nature and wanted to exercise some choice, but could not do that either. In the time of the three great luminaries of painting, Raphael, Correggio, and Titian, painting was finally raised to the level of discrimination, as was sculpture by Michelangelo, and through discrimination taste returned to the arts. But since art is an imitation of the whole of nature, it is too vast for the human mind, and will always be less than perfect in the hands of men. Painters at first differed from one another in their ignorant omission of this element or that, or in making a poor choice from nature. The three luminaries selected certain aspects of nature which they were the first to distinguish. Each of these great masters chose a special aspect, thinking that it was the essence of art. Raphael chose significance, finding it in composition and drawing. Correggio chose grace which he found in certain forms, particularly in light and shade. Titian chose the appearance of truth and

---

[8] The translation is based on Anton Raphael Mengs, *Gedanken über die Schönheit und über den Geschmack in der Malerei*, Leipzig (Reklam), 1876. An early English translation, not used in the text, is available in the form of Chev. Don Joseph Nicholas d'Azara, *The Works of Anthony Raphael Mengs*, London, 1796.

found it chiefly in color. Raphael, therefore, was the greatest of them, for he possessed the greatest part; and since significance is unquestionably the only useful part of painting, Raphael is unquestionably the greatest painter. After this comes grace, which makes Correggio the second greatest painter. Truth, on the other hand, is an obligation, rather than an ornament, hence Titian is the third.

The Two Ways Leading to Correct Taste

There are two ways which lead the rational seeker to good taste; one of these is more difficult than the other. The more difficult is to select the most essential and beautiful from nature itself; the other, easier way is to learn from works of art in which such selection has already taken place.

By the first of these two ways, the ancients found perfection, i.e., beauty and good taste. Most of those who followed after the three luminaries aforementioned (Raphael, Correggio, and Titian) arrived at good taste by the second way. But these three achieved it partly by the first, partly by a compromise of nature and imitation. To achieve good taste through nature is much more difficult than to achieve it through imitation of art, because it requires a philosophical intellect to judge what is good, better, or best in nature, while it is easier to determine this in imitating works of art, since it is easier to understand the works of men than the works of nature. Nevertheless, it is important to use the latter method properly, in order not to get caught up in superficialities and miss the deeper cause of beauty in works of art.

The Education of the Artist

To begin with, the student should consider only the best works, and never tolerate or examine, or even imitate anything ugly. He should copy beautiful works correctly, without questioning at the start the reasons for their beauty. This will train the justness of his eye, the most essential instrument of art. Once he has reached this point, he should begin to examine critically the works of the greatest masters and to inquire into their causes. This is to be done as follows: the painter might examine, for example, all the works of Raphael, Titian, and Correggio, and see what beauties he finds in each work. If in all the works of a particular master he finds certain features consistently well observed and beautifully executed, he can take this as a sign that these features indicate the master's main intention and choice. But if he should find them so in only certain works and not in others, this means that they were not the master's strength and were not part of his intention or taste, and therefore cannot be the reason for the beauty of his work and taste.

Comparison of the Ancients with the Moderns

Nearly all painters have chosen particular specialities in which to attain perfection; the ancients did the same. But all artists since the Renaissance have actually been prompted by a single cause and intent, namely the imitation of nature. This was the main goal toward which they strove along different ways. The ancient Greeks, too, had one main aim, despite their diversity, but this was much more elevated than the aim of the moderns. Since their conceptions were capable of attaining perfection of themselves, they set as their aim the mean between high perfection and humanity, namely beauty, and took only the significant from truth. For this reason, there is beauty in all their works, and even significance is never so much emphasized as to extinguish beauty. I venture therefore to call their taste that of beauty and perfection. Though, being human, their works are imperfect, they nevertheless have the flavor of perfection. Just as wine, even when mixed with water, always retains the flavor of wine, their works, though diminished by their humanity, taste of perfection, for which reason I call them thus. The works of the ancients in fact differ considerably in their quality and significance, but not in their taste. There are three main classes of ancient monuments; in other words, the statues which have been preserved show three degrees of beauty. The least among them still have the taste of beauty, but only in their essential parts. Works of the second grade have beauty in the useful parts as well. Works of the highest grade have beauty in all parts, from the essential to the superfluous, and are therefore perfectly beautiful. Beauty in itself is nothing other than the perfection of every concept, for which reason the most perfect things, invisible as well as visible, are called beautiful. This should guide us in looking at the works of the ancients: their beauty does not always consist of the same part, but lies in the fact that that part which the Idea has chosen has been represented most beautifully. The most beautiful works of the first class are the Laocoon and the Torso, the highest of the second class the Apollo and the Borghese Gladiator, those of the third class are numberless, and of the inferior works I shall not speak at all.

Eclectic Style

I conclude therefore that the painter who wants to discover the good, that is to say, the best taste, must learn about taste from these four: from the ancients the taste for beauty; from Raphael the taste for significance or expression; from Correggio the taste for the graceful or harmonious; from Titian the taste for truth or color. But all of this he must search for in life, for all I have written and explained is intended to give young artists the touchstone for judging their own taste. . . . These exemplars have often been imitated by other great men, but none has surpassed them, which confirms the truth that the great masters who I have named above took the proper road to perfection. This is why I have used them as models and shown the way of understanding and truly imitating them: whoever will exercise his head and hand diligently and reflect on what I have said, will some day take pleasure in his work and effort, and find good taste.

Sir Joshua Reynolds (1723–1792)

On the occasions of the British Royal Academy's distributions of prizes, the President, Sir Joshua Reynolds, was in the habit of presenting formal speeches to the assembled staff and student body. He began in 1769, one year after the foundation of the Academy, and spoke for the last time in 1790, having given fifteen Discourses *in the intervening years. These constitute the most coherent and systematic statement in the English language of the principles of academic training.*

It is important to remember that the institution for which Reynolds spoke was new and had not yet proven itself in England. The confidence which rings in the Discourses *must have been, at least in part, assumed. It was certainly not based on teaching successes, nor was there any substantial body of experience in the doctrine itself. Distilled and strained out of literature, out of the long, plagiaristic pamphleteering tradition, and fed by literati, dilettanti, and antiquarians, its body had only rarely been refreshed by the infusion of practical wisdom from the studio. Few, if any, artists had ever been formed by academic prescriptions. "Raphael, it is true, had not the advantage of studying in an Academy," as Reynolds remarked, but neither had Reynolds or any of his British colleagues. The seeming finality and orderliness of his pronouncements* ex cathedra *show him in his academic robes; but he was also, unlike most Academy presidents, a great painter. As an artist, he was familiar with the doubts which beset the practitioner and which mere theory cannot dispel. This knowledge saved him from schematic dogmatizing, and gave to his* Discourses *the dramatic interest of an inner conflict and a gradual shift of attitude. In the moving praise of Michelangelo with which he concluded his last* Discourse, *he appears on the point of giving way to the "promptings of great and irresistible impulse," in paying tribute to a "divine energy" beyond rules. But despite this final bow to genius, Reynolds throughout the* Discourses *remains steadfast in the conviction that art can be taught, that it is, in other words, a matter of knowledge and application. Success in the arts comes from the conscious observation of principles which, given a normal intelligence and the proper instruction, any person can acquire. In his first* Discourse *he therefore recommends "that an implicit obedience to the Rules of Art, as established by the practice of the great Masters, should be exacted from the young Students; that those models, which have passed through the approbation of ages, should be considered by them as perfect and infallible guides." Intelligent imitation and hard, long study make artists, not enthusiasm or innate talent. Even Raphael was no exception; though he "had not the advantage of studying in an Academy, . . . all Rome, and the works of Michelangelo in particular, were to him an Academy." To which William Blake, a generation later, replied in an angry annotation: "I do not believe that Raphael taught Mich. Angelo, or that Mich. Angelo taught Raphael, any more than I believe that the Rose teaches the Lily how to grow, or the Apple tree teaches the Pear tree how to bear Fruit."*

Sir Joshua Reynolds' Opinion of the Discourses (from *Discourse XV*) [9]

I am truly sensible how unequal I have been to the expression of my own ideas. To develop the latent excellencies, and draw out the interior principles, of our art, requires more skill and practice in writing, than is likely to be possessed by a man perpetually occupied in the use of the pencil and the pallet. It is for that reason, perhaps, that the sister Art has had the advantage of better criticism. Poets are naturally writers of prose. They may be said to be practising only an inferior department of their own art, when they are explaining and expatiating upon its most refined principles. But still such difficulties ought not to deter Artists who are not prevented by other engagements from putting their thoughts in order as well as they can, and from giving to the publick the result of their experience. The knowledge which an Artist has of his subject will more than compensate for any want of elegance in the manner of treating it, or even of perspicuity, which is still more essential; and I am convinced that one short essay written by a Painter, will contribute more to advance the theory of our art, than a thousand volumes such as we sometimes see; the purpose of which appears to be rather to display the refinement of the Author's own conceptions of impossible practice, than to convey useful knowledge or instruction of any kind whatever. An Artist knows what is, and what is not, within the

[9] Sir Joshua Reynolds, *Discourses on Art* (ed. Robert R. Wark), The Huntington Library, San Marino, 1959. The sections quoted will be found under *Discourse III*, pp. 41 ff.; *Discourse V*, pp. 81 ff.; and *Discourse XV*, pp. 267 ff.

province of his art to perform, and is not likely to be for ever teasing the poor Student with the beauties of mixed passions, or to perplex him with an imaginary union of excellencies incompatible with each other. . . .

In reviewing my Discourses, it is no small satisfaction to be assured that I have, in no part of them, lent my assistance to foster *newly hatched unfledged* opinions, or endeavoured to support paradoxes, however tempting may have been their novelty, or however ingenious I might, for the minute, fancy them to be; nor shall I, I hope, any where be found to have imposed on the minds of young Students declamation for argument, a smooth period for a sound precept. I have pursued a plain and *honest method;* I have taken up the art simply as I found it exemplified in the practice of the most approved Painters. That approbation which the world has uniformly given, I have endeavoured to justify by such proofs as questions of this kind will admit; by the analogy which Painting holds with the sister Arts, and consequently by the common congeniality which they all bear to our nature. And though in what has been done, no new discovery is pretended, I may still flatter myself, that from the discoveries which others have made by their own intuitive good sense and native rectitude of judgment, I have succeeded in establishing the rules and principles of our Art on a more firm and lasting foundation than that on which they had formerly been placed.

A central theme which runs through the Discourses *is the discussion of the proper management of the visual forms that nature provides. True to classicist principle, Reynolds warned his listeners against simple imitation, and advocated, instead, a reasoned choice of only the best and most durable forms in nature. He advised artists to cut through the trivial variety of particular, external appearance, in order to enable them to reach the timeless generality of nature's "central form." It was this aspect of his doctrine that drew down on him the most persistent attacks of later critics, and united against him the spokesmen of romanticism and naturalism (see Blake's comments, page 120, the observations of Hazlitt, Vol. II, pp. 91–92, and those of Ruskin, Vol. II, p. 72).*

From *Discourse III: The Great Leading Principles of the Grand Style.—Of Beauty.— The Genuine Habits of Nature to be Distinguished from those of Fashion*

Gentlemen,

The first endeavours of a young Painter, as I have remarked in a former discourse, must be employed in the attainment of mechanical dexterity, and confined to the mere imitation of the object before him. Those who have advanced beyond the rudiments, may, perhaps, find advantage in reflecting on the advice which I have likewise given them, when I recommended the diligent study of the works of our great predecessors; but I at the same time endeavoured to guard them against an implicit submission to the authority of any one master however excellent; or by a strict imitation of his manner, precluding themselves from the abundance and variety of Nature. I will now add that Nature herself is not to be too closely copied. There are excellencies in the art of painting beyond what is commonly called the imitation of nature: and these excellencies I wish to point out. The students who, having passed through the initiatory exercises, are more advanced in the art, and who, sure of their hand, have leisure to exert their understanding, must now be told, that a mere copier of nature can never produce any thing great; can never raise and enlarge the conceptions, or warm the heart of the spectator.

The wish of the genuine painter must be more extensive: instead of endeavouring to amuse mankind with the minute neatness of his imitations, he must endeavour to improve them by the grandeur of his ideas; instead of seeking praise, by deceiving the superficial sense of the spectator, he must strive for fame, by captivating the imagination.

The principle now laid down, that the perfection of this art does not consist in mere imitation, is far from being new or singular. It is, indeed, supported by the general opinion of the enlightened part of mankind. The poets, orators, and rhetoricians of antiquity, are continually enforcing this position; that all the arts receive their perfection from an ideal beauty, superior to what is to be found in individual nature. They are ever referring to the practice of the painters and sculptors of their times, particularly Phidias (the favourite artist of antiquity) to illustrate their assertions. As if they could not sufficiently express their admiration of this genius by what they knew, they have recourse to poetical enthusiasm. They call it inspiration; a gift from heaven. The artist is supposed to have ascended the celestial regions, to furnish his mind with this perfect idea of beauty. "He," says Proclus, "who takes for his model such forms as nature produces, and confines himself to an exact imitation of them, will never attain to what is perfectly beautiful. For the works of nature are full of disproportion, and fall very short of the true standard of beauty. So that Phidias, when he formed his Jupiter, did not copy any object ever presented to his sight; but contemplated only that image which he had conceived in his mind from Homer's description." And thus Cicero, speaking of the same Phidias: "Neither did this artist," says he, "when he carved the image of Jupiter or Minerva, set before him any one human figure, as a pattern, which he was to copy; but having a more perfect idea of beauty fixed in his mind, this he steadily contemplated, and to the imitation of this all his skill and labour were directed."

The Moderns are not less convinced than the Ancients of this superior power existing in the art; nor less sensible of its effects. Every language has adopted terms expressive of this excellence. The *gusto grande* of the Italians, the *beau ideal* of the French, and the *great style, genius,* and *taste* among the English, are but different appellations of the same thing. It is this intellectual dignity, they say, that ennobles the painter's art; that lays the line between him and the mere mechanick; and produces those great effects in an instant, which eloquence and poetry, by slow and repeated efforts, are scarcely able to attain.

Such is the warmth with which both the Ancients and Moderns speak of this divine principle of the art; but, as I have formerly observed, enthusiastick admiration seldom promotes knowledge. Though a student by such praise may have his attention roused, and a desire excited, of running in this great career; yet it is possible that what has been said to excite, may only serve to deter him. He examines his own mind, and perceives there nothing of that divine inspiration, with which, he is told, so many others have been favoured. He never travelled to heaven to gather new ideas; and he finds himself possessed of no other qualifications than what mere common observation and a plain understanding can confer. Thus he becomes gloomy amidst the splendour of figurative declamation, and thinks it hopeless, to pursue an object which he supposes out of the reach of human industry.

But on this, as upon many other occasions, we ought to distinguish how much is to be given to enthusiasm, and how much to reason. We ought to allow for, and we ought to commend, that strength of vivid expression, which is necessary to convey, in its full force, the highest sense of the most complete effect of art; taking care at the same time, not to lose in terms of vague admiration, that solidity and truth of principle, upon which alone we can reason, and may be enabled to practise.

It is not easy to define in what this great style consists; nor to describe, by words, the proper means of acquiring it, if the mind of the student should be at all capable of such an acquisition. Could we teach taste or genius by rules, they would be no longer taste and genius. But though there neither are, nor can be, any precise invariable rules for the exercise, or the acquisition, of these great qualities, yet we may truly say that they always operate in proportion to our attention in observing the works of nature, to our skill in selecting, and to our care in digesting, methodizing, and comparing our observations. There are many beauties in our art, that seem, at first, to lie without the reach of precept, and yet may easily be reduced to practical principles. Experience is all in all; but it is not every one who profits by experience; and most people err, not so much from want of capacity to find their object, as from not knowing what object to pursue. This great ideal perfection and beauty are not to be sought in the heavens, but upon the earth. They are about us, and upon every side of us. But the power of discovering what is deformed in nature, or in other words, what is particular and uncommon, can be acquired only by experience; and the whole beauty and grandeur of the art consists, in my opinion, in being able to get above all singular forms, local customs, particularities, and details of every kind.

All the objects which are exhibited to our view by nature, upon close examination will be found to have their blemishes and defects. The most beautiful forms have something about them like weakness, minuteness, or imperfection. But it is not every eye that perceives these blemishes. It must be an eye long used to the contemplation and comparison of these forms; and which, by a long habit of observing what any set of objects of the same kind have in common, has acquired the power of discerning what each wants in particular. This long laborious comparison should be the first study of the painter, who aims at the greatest style. By this means, he acquires a just idea of beautiful forms; he corrects nature by herself, her imperfect state by her more perfect. His eye being enabled to distinguish the accidental deficiencies, excrescences, and deformities of things, from their general figures, he makes out an abstract idea of their forms more perfect than any one original; and what may seem a paradox, he learns to design naturally by drawing his figures unlike to any one object. This idea of the perfect state of nature, which the Artist calls the Ideal Beauty, is the great leading principle, by which works of genius are conducted. By this Phidias acquired his fame. He wrought upon a sober principle, what has so much excited the enthusiasm of the world; and by this method you, who have courage to tread the same path, may acquire equal reputation.

This is the idea which has acquired, and which seems to have a right to the epithet of *divine;* as it may be said to preside, like a supreme judge, over all the productions of nature; appearing to be possessed of the will and intention of the Creator, as far as they regard the external form of living beings. When a man once possesses this idea in its perfection, there is no danger, but that he will be sufficiently warmed by it himself, and be able to warm and ravish every one else.

Thus it is from a reiterated experience, and a close comparison of the objects in nature, that an artist becomes possessed of the idea of that central form, if I may so express it, from which every deviation is deformity. But the investigation of this form, I grant, is painful, and I know but of one method of shortening the road; this is, by a careful study of the works of the ancient sculptors; who, being indefatigable in the school of nature, have left models of that perfect form behind them, which an artist would prefer as supremely beautiful, who had spent his whole life in that single contemplation. But if industry carried them thus far, may not you also hope for the same reward from the same labour? We have the same school opened to us, that was opened to them; for nature denies her instructions to none, who desire to become her pupils.

This laborious investigation, I am aware, must appear superfluous to those who think every thing is to be done by felicity, and the powers of native genius. Even the great Bacon treats with ridicule the idea of confining proportion to rules, or of producing beauty by selection. "A man cannot tell," says he, "whether Apelles or Albert Dürer were the more trifler: whereof the one would make a personage by geometrical proportions; the other, by taking the best parts out of divers faces, to make one excellent. . . . The painter, [he adds], must do it by a kind of felicity, . . . and not by rule."

It is not safe to question any opinion of so great a writer, and so profound a thinker, as undoubtedly Bacon was. But he studies brevity to excess; and therefore his meaning is sometimes doubtful. If he means that beauty has nothing to do with rule, he is mistaken. There is a rule, obtained out of general nature, to contradict which is to fall into deformity. Whenever any thing is done beyond this rule, it is in virtue of some other rule which is followed along with it, but which does not contradict it. Every thing which is wrought with certainty, is wrought upon some principle. If it is not, it cannot be repeated. If by felicity is meant any thing of chance or hazard, or something born with a man, and not earned, I cannot agree with this great philosopher. Every object which pleases must give us pleasure upon some certain principles; but as the objects of pleasure are almost infinite, so their principles vary without end, and every man finds them out, not by felicity or successful hazard, but by care and sagacity.

To the principle I have laid down, that the idea of beauty in each species of beings is an invariable one, it may be objected, that in every particular species there are various central forms, which are separate and distinct from each other, and yet are undeniably beautiful; that in the human figure, for instance, the beauty of Hercules is one, of the Gladiator another, of the Apollo another; which makes so many different ideas of beauty.

It is true, indeed, that these figures are each perfect in their kind, though of different characters and proportions; but still none of them is the representation of an individual, but of a class. And as there is one general form, which, as I have said, belongs to the human kind at large, so in each of these classes there is one common idea and central form, which is the abstract of the various individual forms belonging to that class. Thus, though the forms of childhood and age differ exceedingly, there is a common form in childhood, and a common form in age, which is the more perfect, as it is more remote from all peculiarities. But I must add further, that though the most perfect forms of each of the general divisions of the human figure are ideal, and superior to any individual form of that class; yet the highest perfection of the human figure is not to be found in any one of them. It is not in the Hercules, nor in the Gladiator, nor in the Apollo; but in that form which is taken from them all, and which partakes equally of the activity of the Gladiator, of the delicacy of the Apollo, and of the muscular strength of the Hercules. For perfect beauty in any species must combine all the characters which are beautiful in that species. It cannot consist in any one to the exclusion of the rest: no one, therefore, must be predominant, that no one may be deficient.

The knowledge of these different characters, and the power of separating and distinguishing them, is undoubtedly necessary to the painter, who is to vary his compositions with figures of various forms and proportions, though he is never to lose sight of the general idea of perfection in each kind.

There is, likewise, a kind of symmetry, or proportion, which may properly be said to belong to deformity. A figure lean or corpulent, tall or short, though deviating from beauty, may still have a certain union of the various parts, which may contribute to make them on the whole not unpleasing.

When the Artist has by diligent attention acquired a clear and distinct idea of beauty and symmetry; when he has reduced the variety of nature to the abstract idea; his next task will be to become acquainted with the genuine habits of nature, as distinguished from those of fashion. For in the same manner, and on the same principles, as he has acquired the knowledge of the real forms of nature, distinct from accidental deformity, he must endeavour to separate simple chaste nature, from those adventitious, those affected and forced airs or actions, with which she is loaded by modern education.

However the mechanick and ornamental arts may sacrifice to fashion, she must be entirely excluded from the Art of Painting; the painter must never mistake this capricious changeling for the genuine offspring of nature; he must divest himself of all prejudices in favour of his age or country; he must disregard all local and temporary ornaments, and look only on those general habits which are every where and always the same. He addresses his works to the people of every country and every age; he calls upon posterity to be his spectators, and says with Zeuxis, *in æternitatem pingo.*

The neglect of separating modern fashions from the habits of nature, leads to that ridiculous style which has been practised by some painters, who have given to Grecian Heroes the airs and graces practised in the court of Lewis the Fourteenth; an absurdity almost as great as it would have been to have dressed them after the fashion of that court.

To avoid this error, however, and to retain the true simplicity of nature, is a task more difficult than at first sight it may appear. The prejudices in favour of the fashions and customs that we have been used to, and which are justly called a second nature, make it too often difficult to distinguish that which is natural, from that which is the result of education; they frequently even give a predilection in favour of the artificial mode; and almost every one is apt to be guided by those local prejudices, who has not chastised his mind, and regulated the instability of his affections by the eternal invariable idea of nature.

Here then, as before, we must have recourse to the Ancients as instructors. It is from a careful study of their works that you will be enabled to attain to the real simplicity of nature; they will suggest many observations, which would probably escape you, if your study were confined to nature alone. And, indeed, I cannot help suspecting, that in this instance the ancients had an easier task than the moderns. They had, probably, little or nothing to unlearn, as their manners were nearly approaching to this desirable simplicity; while the modern artist, before he can see the truth of things, is obliged to remove a veil, with which the fashion of the times has thought proper to cover her.

Having gone thus far in our investigation of the great stile in painting; if we now should suppose that the artist has formed the true idea of beauty, which enables him to give his works a correct and perfect design; if we should suppose also, that he has acquired a knowledge of the unadulterated habits of nature, which gives him simplicity; the rest of his task is, perhaps, less than is generally imagined. Beauty and simplicity have so great a share in the composition of a great stile, that he who has acquired them has little else to learn. It must not, indeed, be forgotten, that there is a nobleness of conception, which goes beyond any thing in the mere exhibition even of perfect form; there is an art of animating and dignifying the figures with intellectual grandeur, of impressing the appearance of philosophick wisdom, or heroick virtue. This can only be acquired by him that enlarges the sphere of his understanding by a variety of knowledge, and warms his imagination with the best productions of ancient and modern poetry.

A hand thus exercised, and a mind thus instructed, will bring the art to an higher degree of excellence than, perhaps, it has hitherto attained in this country. Such a student will disdain the humbler walks of painting, which, however profitable, can never assure him a permanent reputation. He will leave the meaner artist servilely to suppose that those are the best pictures, which are most likely to deceive the spectator. He will permit the lower painter, like the florist or collector of shells, to exhibit the minute discriminations, which distinguish one object of the same species from another; while he, like the philosopher, will consider nature in the abstract, and represent in every one of his figures the character of its species.

If deceiving the eye were the only business of the art, there is no doubt, indeed, but the minute painter would be more apt to succeed: but it is not the eye, it is the mind, which the painter of genius desires to address; nor will he waste a moment upon those smaller objects, which only serve to catch the sense, to divide the attention, and to counteract his great design of speaking to the heart.

This is the ambition which I wish to excite in your minds; and the object I have had in my view, throughout this discourse, is that one great idea, which gives to painting its true dignity, which entitles it to the name of a Liberal Art, and ranks it as a sister of poetry.

It may possibly have happened to many young students, whose application was sufficient to overcome all difficulties, and whose minds were capable of embracing the most extensive views, that they have, by a wrong direction originally given, spent their lives in the meaner walks of painting, without ever knowing there was a nobler to pursue. Albert Dürer, as Vasari has justly remarked, would, probably, have been one of the first painters of his age (and he lived in an era of great artists), had he been initiated into those great principles of the art, which were so well understood and practised by his contemporaries in Italy. But unluckily having never seen or heard of any other manner, he, without doubt, considered his own as perfect.

As for the various departments of painting, which do not presume to make such high pretensions, they are many. None of them are without their merit, though none enter into competition with this universal presiding idea of the art. The painters who have applied themselves more particularly to low and vulgar characters, and who express with precision the various shades of passion, as they are exhibited by vulgar minds (such as we see in the works of Hogarth), deserve great praise; but as their genius has been employed on low and confined subjects, the praise which we give must be as limited as its object. The merry-making, or quarrelling, of the Boors of Teniers; the same sort of productions of Brouwer, or Ostade, are excellent in their kind; and the excellence and its praise will be in proportion, as, in those limited subjects, and peculiar forms, they introduce more or less of the expression of those passions, as they appear in general and more enlarged nature. This principle may be applied to the Battle-pieces of Bourgognone, the French Gallantries of Watteau, and even beyond the exhibition of animal life, to the Landscapes of Claude Lorrain, and the Sea-Views of Vandervelde. All these painters have, in general, the same right, in different degrees, to the name of a painter, which a satirist, an epigrammatist, a sonneteer, a writer of pastorals, or descriptive poetry, has to that of a poet.

In the same rank, and perhaps of not so great merit, is the cold painter of portraits. But his correct and just imitation of his object has its merit. Even the painter of still life, whose highest ambition is to give a minute representation of every part of those low objects which he sets before him, deserves praise in proportion to his attainment; because no part of this excellent art, so much the ornament of polished life, is destitute of value and use. These, however, are by no means the views to which the mind of the student ought to be *primarily* directed. Having begun by aiming at better things, if from particular inclination, or from the taste of the time and place he lives in, or from necessity, or from failure in the highest attempts, he is obliged to descend lower, he will bring into the lower sphere of art a grandeur of composition and character, that will raise and ennoble his works far above their natural rank.

A man is not weak, though he may not be able to wield the club of Hercules; nor does a man always practise that which he esteems the best; but does that which he can best do. In moderate attempts, there are many walks open to the artist. But as the idea of beauty is of necessity but one, so there can be but one great mode of painting; the leading principle of which I have endeavoured to explain.

I should be sorry, if what is here recommended, should be at all understood to countenance a careless or indetermined manner of painting. For though the painter is to overlook the accidental discriminations of nature, he is to exhibit distinctly, and with precision, the general forms of things. A firm and determined outline is one of the characteristics of the great style in painting; and let me add, that he who possesses the knowledge of the exact form which every part of nature ought to have, will be fond of expressing that knowledge with correctness and precision in all his works.

Raphael and Michaelangelo Compared (from *Discourse V*)

Raphael, who stands in general foremost of the first painters, owes his reputation, as I have observed, to his excellence in the higher parts of the art: his works in *Fresco,* therefore, ought to be the first object of our study and attention. His *easel*-works stand in a lower degree of estimation; for though he continually, to the day of his death, embellished his performances more and more with the addition of those lower ornaments, which entirely make the merit of some painters, yet he never arrived at such perfection as to make him an object of imitation. He never was able to conquer perfectly that dryness, or even littleness of manner, which he inherited from his master. He never acquired that nicety of taste in colours, that breadth of light and shadow, that art and management of uniting light to light, and shadow to shadow, so as to make the object rise out of the ground with that plenitude of effect so much admired in the works of Correggio. When he painted in oil, his hand seemed to be so cramped and confined, that he not only lost that facility and spirit, but I think even that correctness of form, which is so perfect and admirable in his *Fresco*-works. I do not recollect any pictures of his of this kind, except perhaps the Transfiguration, in which there are not some parts that appear to be even feebly drawn. That this is not a necessary attendant on Oil-painting, we have abundant instances in more modern painters. Lodovico Carracci, for instance, preserved in his works in oil the same spirit, vigour, and correctness, which he had in *Fresco*. I have no desire to degrade Raphael from the high rank which he deservedly holds; but by comparing him with himself, he does not appear to me to be the same man in Oil as in Fresco.

From those who have ambition to tread in this great walk of the art, Michael Angelo claims the next attention. He did not possess so many excellencies as Raphael, but those which he had were of the highest kind. He considered the art as consisting of little more than what may be attained by Sculpture; correctness of form, and energy of character. We ought not to expect more than an artist intends in his work. He never attempted those lesser elegancies and graces in the art. Vasari says, he never painted but one picture in oil, and resolved never to paint another, saying, it was an employment only fit for women and children.

If any man had a right to look down upon the lower accomplishments as beneath his attention, it was certainly Michael Angelo; nor can it be thought strange, that such a mind should have slighted or have been withheld from paying due attention to all those graces and embellishments of art, which have diffused such lustre over the works of other painters.

It must be acknowledged, however, that together with these, which we wish he had more attended to, he has rejected all the false, though specious ornaments, which disgrace the works even of the most esteemed artists; and I will venture to say, that when those higher excellencies are more known and cultivated by the artists and the patrons of arts, his fame and credit will increase with our increasing knowledge. His name will then be held in the same veneration as it was in the enlightened age of Leo the tenth: and it is remarkable that the reputation of this truly great man has been continually declining as the art itself has declined. For I must remark to you, that it has long been much on the decline, and that our only hope of its revival will consist in your being thoroughly sensible of its depravation and decay. It is to Michael Angelo, that we owe even the existence of Raphael: it is to him Raphael owes the grandeur of his style. He was taught by him to elevate his thoughts, and to conceive his subjects with dignity. His genius, however formed to blaze and to shine, might, like fire in combustible matter, for ever have lain dormant, if it had not caught a spark by its contact with Michael Angelo: and though it never burst out with *his* extraordinary heat and vehemence, yet it must be acknowledged to be a more pure, regular, and chaste flame. Though our judgement must upon the whole decide in favour of Raphael, yet he never takes such a firm hold and entire possession of the mind as to make us desire nothing else, and to feel nothing wanting. The effect of the capital works of Michael Angelo perfectly corresponds to what Bouchardon said he felt from reading Homer; his whole frame appeared to himself to be enlarged, and all nature which surrounded him, diminished to atoms.

If we put these great artists in a light of comparison with each other, Raphael had more Taste and Fancy, Michael Angelo more Genius and Imagination. The one excelled in beauty, the other in energy. Michael Angelo has more of the Poetical Inspiration; his ideas are vast and sublime; his people are a superior order of beings; there is nothing about them, nothing in the air of their actions or their attitudes, or the style and cast of their limbs or features, that reminds us of their belonging to our own species. Raphael's imagination is not so elevated; his figures are not so much disjoined from our own diminutive race of beings, though his ideas are chaste, noble, and of great conformity to their subjects. Michael Angelo's works have a strong, peculiar, and marked character: they seem to proceed from his own mind entirely, and that mind so rich and abundant, that he never needed, or seemed to disdain, to look abroad for foreign help. Raphael's materials are generally borrowed, though the noble structure is his own. The excellency of this extraordinary man lay in the propriety, beauty, and majesty of his characters, the judicious contrivance of his Composition, his correctness of Drawing, purity of Taste, and skilful accommodation of other men's conceptions to his own purpose. Nobody excelled him in that judgement, with which he united to his own observations on Nature, the Energy of Michael Angelo, and the Beauty and Simplicity of the Antique. To the question therefore, which ought to hold the first rank, Raphael or Michael Angelo, it must be answered, that if it is to be given to him who possessed a greater combination of the higher qualities of the art than any other man, there is no doubt but Raphael is the first. But if, as Longinus thinks, the sublime, being the highest excellence that human composition can attain to, abundantly compensates the absence of every other beauty, and atones for all other deficiencies, then Michael Angelo demands the preference.

The Sublimity of Michaelangelo, Last Words Pronounced by Sir Joshua Reynolds from the Presidential Chair of the Academy (from *Discourse XV*)

I would ask any man qualified to judge of such works, whether he can look with indifference at the personification of the Supreme Being in the center of the Capella Sestina, or the figures of the Sybils which surround that chapel, to which we may add the statue of Moses; and whether the same sensations are not excited by those works, as what he may remember to have felt from the most sublime passages of Homer?

The sublime in Painting, as in Poetry, so overpowers, and takes such a possession of the whole mind, that no room is left for attention to minute criticism. The little elegancies of art in the presence of these great ideas thus greatly expressed, lose all their value, and are, for the instant at least, felt to be unworthy of our notice. The correct judgment, the purity of taste, which characterise Raphael, the exquisite grace of Correggio and Parmegiano, all disappear before them.

That Michael Angelo was capricious in his inventions, cannot be denied; and this may make some circumspection necessary in studying his works; for though they appear to become him, an imitation of them is always dangerous, and will prove sometimes ridiculous. "Within that circle none durst walk but he." To me, I confess, his caprice does not lower the estimation of his genius, even though it is sometimes, I acknowledge, carried to the extreme: and however those eccentrick excursions are considered, we must at the same time recollect, that those faults, if they are faults, are such as never could occur to a mean and vulgar mind; that they flowed from the same source which produced his greatest beauties, and were therefore such as none but himself was capable of committing; they were the powerful impulses of a mind unused to subjection of any kind, and too high to be controlled by cold criticism.

It must be remembered, that as this great style itself is artificial in the highest degree, it presupposes in the spectator, a cultivated and prepared artificial state of mind. It is an absurdity therefore to suppose that we are born with this taste, though we are with the seeds of it, which, by the heat and kindly influence of his genius, may be ripened in us.

The style of Michael Angelo, which I have compared to language, and which may, poetically speaking, be called the language of the

Gods, now no longer exists, as it did in the fifteenth century; yet, with the aid of diligence, we may in a great measure supply the deficiency which I mentioned, of not having his works so perpetually before our eyes, by having recourse to casts from his models and designs in Sculpture; to drawings or even copies of those drawings; to prints, which however ill executed, still convey something by which this taste may be formed; and a relish may be fixed and established in our minds for this grand style of invention.

I have endeavoured to stimulate the ambition of Artists to tread in this great path of glory, and, as well as I can, have pointed out the track which leads to it, and have at the same time told them the price at which it may be obtained. It is an ancient saying, that labour is the price which the Gods have set upon every thing valuable.

The great Artist, who has been so much the subject of the present Discourse, was distinguished even from his infancy for his indefatigable diligence; and this was continued through his whole life, till prevented by extreme old age. The poorest of men, as he observed himself, did not labour from necessity, more than he did from choice. Indeed, from all the circumstances related of his life, he appears not to have had the least conception that his art was to be acquired by any other means than by great labour; and yet he, of all men that ever lived, might make the greatest pretensions to the efficacy of native genius and inspiration. I have no doubt that he would have thought it no disgrace, that it should be said of him, as he himself said of Raphael, that he did not possess his art from nature, but by long study. He was conscious that the great excellence to which he arrived was gained by dint of labour, and was unwilling to have it thought that any transcendent skill, however natural its effects might seem, could be purchased at a cheaper price than he had paid for it.

If the high esteem and veneration in which Michael Angelo has been held by all nations and in all ages, should be put to the account of prejudice, it must still be granted that those prejudices could not have been entertained without a cause: the ground of our prejudice then becomes the source of our admiration. But from whatever it proceeds, or whatever it is called, it will not I hope, be thought presumptuous in me to appear in the train, I cannot say of his imitators, but of his admirers. I have taken another course, one more suited to my abilities, and to the taste of the times in which I live. Yet however unequal I feel myself to that attempt, were I now to begin the world again, I would tread in the steps of that great master: to kiss the hem of his garment, to catch the slightest of his perfections, would be glory and distinction enough for an ambitious man.

I feel a self-congratulation in knowing myself capable of such sensations as he intended to excite. I reflect not without vanity, that these Discourses bear testimony of my admiration of that truly divine man, and I should desire that the last words which I should pronounce in this Academy, and from this place, might be the name of—MICHAEL ANGELO.

Salomon Gessner (1730–1788)

The Swiss poet and painter, Salomon Gessner, literally followed the precept of "ut pictura poesis" in his work: his Arcadian poems read like evocations of the paintings of Claude Lorrain, while his landscape etchings breathe the spirit of Theocritus. Gessner's mild classicism was tinged with a delight in the cozy and quaint which today seems more Rococo, or Swiss, than Hellenic. His Death of Abel *(1758) had an international success; contemporary readers enjoyed its sense of unspoiled nature and quiet grace, qualities which can still be felt in the delicate and naïve illustrations which he drew for his works. The* Letter to Mr. Fuesslin on Landscape Painting *(1770), from which the following excerpts are taken, gives an account of Gessner's self-training as an artist. It is surprising to find that, without external compulsion, he voluntarily administered to himself the eclectic disciplines of the Academy, and attempted to adapt to landscape the Mengsian recipe of imitating and combining the particular styles of diverse masters (see page 30). The* Letter *enjoyed a popularity which extended throughout Europe and continued into the 19th century. Constable and other English artists read it in the very defective translation by W. Hooper (1776) which has not been used for the following excerpts:* [10]

From *Letter to Mr. Fuesslin on Landscape Painting* (1770)

My passion for art reawakened, and I resolved, already thirty years old, to see whether I could still reach the point at which I should gain the respect of connoisseurs and artists.

My predilection was for landscape, and I began by drawing diligently. But something happened to me which has happened to many others before: convinced that nature was the best and truest guide of art, I drew exclusively from nature. What difficulties I had, lacking the facility of seizing the various characteristic expressions in landscape subjects, a facility which can be gained only through the study of the best

[10] The text used in the present translation follows "Brief an Herrn Fuesslin ueber die Landschaftsmalerey," in Salomon Gessner's *Schriften*, Zurich, 1772, V, 3 ff. An early and quite inaccurate English translation is to be found in W. Hooper, *New Idylles by Gessner*, London, 1776.

models. I was too intent on following nature closely, and got bogged down in petty details which hurt the effect of the whole. I nearly always missed the right way of rendering the true character of natural objects without servility or timidity. My foregrounds were cluttered with complex and trivial forms, my trees were timidly drawn and not well ordered in their main masses; tasteless overwork rendered everything disharmonious. In a word, I had not yet trained my eye to see nature as a picture, and had not learned at what point the limitations of art require that something be added or taken away from nature. Thus I discovered that, in order to train myself, I must first follow the best artists. My experience recalls the mistake into which early artists fell when, lacking good examples, they tried to raise art up from its infancy: they kept so close to nature that they often showed the merest accessories as distinctly as the main features. In a later period, artists of genius recognized this fault and tried to avoid it by familiarizing themselves with the rules of beauty in the disposition and variety of masses, in the arrangement of shadow and light, and so forth.

I decided to follow their example, and to shorten my road, I chose only the best work for my models, only those which were excellent in every way. This careful concentration on the very best ought to be a prime rule for every teacher and student. Nothing is more harmful than mediocrity; we should avoid it more carefully than the simply bad which is easier to recognize. . . .

I found it advantageous in my studies to go from one problem to the next. Those who try to do everything at once have chosen a laborious way; their attention is scattered, and they grow tired from having encountered too many obstacles at once. To begin with, I tried trees, and chose Waterloo as my particular model. . . . The more I studied him, the more I discovered true nature in his landscapes. I practiced his manner until I easily mastered it in designs of my own. Meanwhile I did not neglect to copy other artists whose manner is unlike Waterloo's, but who, nonetheless, are felicitous in their imitation of nature. I exercised after Swanevelt and Berghem, and whenever I found a tree or shrub which particularly attracted my attention, I made a rapid sketch of it. By means of these varied exercises, I gained facility of expression and developed a more individual manner than I had got from following Waterloo. I went on, bit by bit. For rocks I chose the large masses to be found in Berghem and Salvator Rosa; for the truly characteristic aspects of nature, the designs of Felix Meyer, Ermels and Hackert; for folds of terrain, Claude's grassy plains and crepuscular distances, or the flowing undulations of receding hills in Wouvermann which look like velvet when soft light touches their grassy surface; and in the end I returned to Waterloo whose grounds are exactly as he found them in his region:

wholly natural, and therefore difficult to imitate. For sandy or rocky areas overgrown with scattered shrubs, grasses or weeds, I chose Berghem.

How much easier the study of nature now became for me! Having learned to recognize what is peculiar to art, I was now infinitely better able to observe nature and to achieve a suggestive manner whenever plain representation was insufficient. During walks I had formerly often looked in vain for something to draw. Now I always discover something along the way. I may not find a tree which is picturesquely beautiful in all its form, but with an eye accustomed to discovery, I can find even in a bad tree some particular detail, some well-shaped branches, a beautiful cluster of foliage, or a single patch of bark which, if I use them sensibly, will give my work truth and beauty. A pebble can suggest the bulk of a rock: it is in my power to hold it up to the light and to observe on it the most beautiful effects of light and shade, half-shadow, and reflection. . . .

But my landscapes still lacked greatness, nobility, and harmony: their illumination was still too scattered, they lacked a vigorous general effect. I had to find a better way of giving them unity.

From among all the artists of the past, I chose those who seemed to me to be the best with respect to ideas, selection, and disposition. I found simple rusticity in Everdingen's landscapes, among sites which are nevertheless extremely varied . . . Swanevelt's noble thoughts . . . Salvator Rosa's bold wildness; Rubens' audacity in the choice of his sites —these and others I studied in rapid drawings, emphasizing the total effect, since I wanted to give free rein to the imagination. Finally, I limited myself entirely to the two Poussins and to Claude Lorrain. In them, I found true greatness: theirs is no simple imitation of nature. . . . In the two Poussins, poetic genius unites all that is grand and noble. They transport us into periods which history and the poets have made us revere and into countries where nature is not wild, but grandiose in its variety, and where, in a benign climate, every plant attains its healthiest perfection. Their buildings have the beautiful simplicity of ancient architecture, and their inhabitants a noble aspect and demeanor, such as our imagination tells us the Greeks and Romans possessed. . . . Grace and contentment prevail in the regions which Lorrain has painted for us: they awaken the same enthusiasm and calm emotion which is aroused by the contemplation of nature itself. They are rich, without being wild or unquiet, varied yet marked by gentleness and repose. His landscapes are prospects of a happy land in which men live in abundance. . . .

I have one further important recommendation for artists: poetry is the true sister of painting. Do not neglect the best works of the poets; they will refine and elevate your taste and ideas, and furnish your imagination with the most beautiful pictures. Both poetry and painting search for the beautiful and grand in nature; they both follow similar laws. Variety without confusion governs the design of their works, and a sensitivity to the truly beautiful guides both in the choice of every circumstance, in every picture, throughout the whole of their work. Many artists would choose nobler subjects, and with more taste. Many poets would give more truth, more picturesque expression to their images, if they combined the knowledge of both arts.

COMMON SENSE AND SENSIBILITY

The rise of lay criticism in the late 18th century resulted in part from the widespread belief that artists, like scientists or moral philosophers, must search for objective truth in the verifiable experience of physical nature or human nature. The Academy's claim that art can be learned through rule and method rested on this belief; it implied that the artist's work was a rational pursuit of attainable social ends—not a form of sorcery or a spontaneous overflowing of mental energy. But a further implication, not so happily acknowledged by Academicians, was that any man of sound mind and feeling can judge the essential value of art, namely its truth, regardless of how ignorant of technical matters he might be. For if art had to stand the test of common sense and common feeling, the intelligent layman had as much right to apply the test as the professional artist, the philosopher, or the historian.

Jean-Étienne Liotard (1702–1789) and the "Ignorart"

In his old age, the Swiss portrait painter and pastellist, Liotard, nicknamed le peintre Turc *because of his travels in the Levant and his bizarre affectation of Turkish costume and beard, wrote a handbook for painters,* Traité des principes et des règles de la peinture *(1781), in which he claimed that ignorant laymen are the best critics of art.*[11]

From Traité des principes et des règles de la peinture

You should not disregard, but rather consider with care, the criticism of your work by people who know nothing about art: there is always some truth in their observations.

This idea may at first strike you as paradoxical, but you will discover

[11] Liotard's text is published in E. Humbert and A. Revilliod, *La vie et les oeuvres de Jean-Étienne Liotard,* Amsterdam, 1897, pp. 86 ff.

on further reflection that it is true. The reason is simple: the painter works from models which nature offers him. This great book is open to all men. It is not surprising that an artist should neglect some of the innumerable details which it contains, and that this omission should immediately strike the eye of the *ignorart*.

This is the name I apply to men who have never drawn or painted, and who know nothing about painting. I want to prove that the *ignorart* is sometimes a very good judge, and that his judgments about art are often preferable to those of the artists themselves. Those who judge best in matters of truth are surely the best judges. Painters are judges of art. The *ignorart* knows nothing about that, but he knows truth and is a judge of truth. Painters judge truth by the standards of art, and often by the standards of art misunderstood. This keeps them from having a sound judgment of truth, as I shall show by means of striking examples.

The *ignorart* has a very exact idea of everything to be found in nature . . . nearly all painters base their judgment on their own manner of painting: this is perfectly understandable; if they did not think their manner the best, they would change it. That is why they are always ready to condemn others whose manner is contrary to theirs. French painters and some of the Flemings love inventive, facile, spontaneous work. Certain Flemings and Dutchmen put all their pride into giving their pictures the most minute finish. The Italians prefer artists who paint in a broad and handsome manner.

I have heard painters give judgments on art which were false to the point of being ridiculous. While looking at a collection of Flemish and Dutch paintings of the highest quality and finish, including works by Gerard Dou, Mieris, Adrian and Willem Van de Velde, Van der Heyde, Ostade, Wouvermans, Van der Werff, Rembrandt, Rubens, Teniers, and other good painters, one of the most accomplished painters in Rome once said to me: "I find no merit in any of these pictures."

An *ignorart* enters the shop of an art merchant in Paris. He finds a female portrait by Rembrandt next to a *Flora,* a mediocre copy by Coypel. The *Flora* gives him more pleasure than Rembrandt's portrait . . . whose face and hands seem to be covered with scars or the marks of smallpox. A painter of his acquaintance tells him: "Look at this beautiful Rembrandt; never mind that worthless *Flora*." The *ignorart,* looking more closely at Rembrandt's work, answered: "It does seem to me that this picture has strength, since it is so brown. Is there some special merit in this vigor and brownness? Did Rembrandt mix soot with his colors? And why has he given his picture these scars and pockmarks?" Shrugging his shoulders, the painter replied: "I can see that you know nothing about painting. How could you imagine that a great artist would mix soot with his colors? Old age has darkened them, but I can still see them under these layers of brown, still beautiful, fresh and true . . . these scars and so-called pockmarks are bold and deliberate touches of the brush which express the softness of flesh, and give vigor, truth, and life to this incomparable picture."

The *ignorart* admits that he is wrong, realizing that he knows nothing about painting, and yet his judgment is true. . . . The painter's judgment is colored by his preoccupation with art. Art, misunderstood, triumphs over truth, as with the country lawyer who persuades a peasant that he is wrong, when the peasant in fact is right. . . .

. . . As for my own work, what truth is to be found in it, I cheerfully confess to all my colleagues, I owe to the *ignorart* who often brought me back to truth when I had lost the way. . . .

Do you believe that those famous, biennial exhibitions at the Louvre are intended merely to flatter the artists of the capital, by way of reward for their labors, and to earn them public admiration and applause? Without fear of being contradicted by the gentlemen of the Royal Academy who might read this, I should say, rather, that added to the perfectly natural desire for public approbation, there is another motive, namely the desire to profit from the criticism of a population which has an innate taste for all the arts, and which possesses a fine sense of their beauties and defects.

Denis Diderot (1713–1784)

Diderot turned to art criticism relatively late in his career. When, in 1759, the publicist F. M. Grimm asked him to contribute a review of the current Salon to the Correspondance littéraire, *the periodic manuscript newsletter which Grimm edited for princely subscribers in Germany, Poland, and Russia, Diderot was still without experience in this field. He had exercised his talent as philosopher, novelist, and dramatist, and had for nearly a decade contributed a great variety of articles to the* Encyclopédie, *but, aside from a treatise on ancient encaustic painting and a fairly abstruse article on Beauty (1751), he had not written on questions of art. From 1759 onward, he regularly reviewed the biennial Paris Salons—in 1761, 1763, 1765, 1767, 1769, and 1771, then, after a longer interval, in 1775, and once again in 1781. It was Grimm's commission which opened his eyes and mind to the work of modern artists and caused him to become a practical critic, rather than a theorist of art. "The task you gave me," he wrote in the Introduction to his* Salon of

1765, "has made me fasten my eyes on the canvas and to walk round the marble. I have given my impressions the time to form and to register. I have opened my mind to visual effects and allowed them to sink in. . . . I have learned to understand subtlety of design and truth to nature. I have experienced the magic of light and shadow. I have understood color and acquired feeling for flesh. I have meditated in solitude on what I have seen and heard, and such terms of art as unity, variety, contrast, symmetry, arrangement, composition, character, expression, so ready to come to my lips, but so vague in my mind, have taken on firm definition."

Journalistic criticism of art and periodic reviews of exhibitions were no longer a novelty when Diderot began. La Font de Saint Yenne (1747), Saint Yves (1748), Count Caylus (1750), Fréron, and Grimm himself had preceded him and had helped to create the type which he was to perfect. Many artists of the period resented the intrusion of lay critics, considering it as a form of charlatanry and a threat to their trade. Others, such as the painter J. E. Liotard, held the paradoxical view that the ignorant made the best critics, since their minds were free of prejudice. Diderot himself was anxious to make up for his practical inexperience by consulting the artists and observing their practice. He listened to de La Tour, Chardin, Greuze, Michel van Loo, and Joseph Vernet, he read copiously, and occasionally appropriated the thoughts of others.

His reviews, written under the impact of fresh impressions, are very little burdened with abstract theory. The basis of his judgments was a secular morality which, without clear differentiation between ethics and aesthetics, put a high value on the socially useful, the instructive, and the elevating. He accepted as a matter of common sense that art must follow nature and that to deviate from nature was to fall into error or vice. The artist must discover in external and in human nature the special qualities and correspondences of form and feeling which constitute the truth of art. This truth was not primarily a matter of visual resemblance, but of psychological and moral rightness, and its proof lay in the response of the sensibility, the verdict of the uncorrupted heart. Given this approach, it is not surprising that Diderot's "nature" should strike the modern reader as heavily moralized and overlaid with literary artifice. His descriptions of paintings stress narrative, arrangement, and situation, and sometimes read like scenarios. His bias, reflecting his espousal of contemporary attitudes, kept him from doing justice to Boucher and made him admire the moralized landscapes of Vernet and the sentimental genres of Greuze. But Diderot had too sound an instinct and too much keenness of eye to fall victim to the momentarily interesting. As he gained assurance and experience, the essential pictorial elements in art, particularly light and color, began to preoccupy him more

*and more, and in time led him to value the painterly genius of Chardin
over the seductive rhetoric of Greuze.*[12]

Francois Boucher, "Shepherd Scene," (Salon of 1763)

Imagine, in the background, a vase standing on a pedestal and
crowned with bundled branches. Place beneath it a shepherd, asleep with
his head on the knees of his shepherdess. Scatter about them a shepherd's
crook, a little hat filled with roses, a dog, some sheep, a bit of landscape,
and Heaven knows how many more details, all piled on top of one
another; then paint the whole in the most brilliant colors, and you'll
have the *Shepherd Scene* of Boucher.

What a waste of talent and of time! Half the effort would have
produced twice the effect. The eye rambles among so many objects, all
rendered with equal care; there is no sense of atmosphere, no quiet. Yet
the shepherdess has the look of her kind, and the bit of landscape
squeezed in near the vase has a surprising delicacy, freshness, and
charm. But what does this vase and pedestal mean? What are these heavy
branches which top it? Must a writer say all? Must a painter paint everything? Can't he leave anything at all to my imagination? But just try to
suggest this to a man who has been spoiled by praise and who is obsessed
by his talent; he'll shrug disdainfully, he'll ignore you, and we'll leave
him to himself—he is condemned to love only himself and his works. It's
a pity, though.

For when this man had just returned from Italy he painted beautifully, his colors were strong and true, his compositions well thought out
and yet full of intensity, his execution was broad and impressive. I know
some of his earliest pictures which he now calls daubs and would like
to buy back in order to burn them.

He has some old portfolios full of admirable works which he now
despises. And he has some new ones, all dolled up with sheep and shepherds in the manner of Fontenelle, over which he gloats.

This man is the ruin of our young painting students. As soon as

---

12 Diderot's writings on art are contained in their entirety in J. Assézat (editor),
Oeuvres complètes de Diderot, Paris, 1876, vols. X–XIII. From this source were derived
the translation of the excerpts from the *Essays on Painting* and the *Pensées detachées
sur la peinture.* The *Salons* are being separately published in a new edition by J. Seznec
and Jean Adhémar (Oxford, 1957–1963). The entries concerning Boucher and Chardin
were translated from Vol. I (pp. 202 and 222 respectively) of Seznec and Adhémar's
publication which comprises the Salons of 1759, 1761, and 1763, while Vol. II is devoted to the Salon of 1765, and Vol. III to the Salon of 1767. The translation of
Diderot's description of Greuze's "Ungrateful Son" was taken from Lester G. Crocker
(ed.) and Derek Coltman (trans.), *Diderot's Selected Writings,* New York, © The Macmillan Company, 1966, p. 150. Quoted by permission of the publisher.

they are able to hold brush and palette, they begin to sweat over garlanded putti, to paint rosy and dimpled behinds, and to indulge in all sorts of extravagances which are not saved by the warmth, originality, prettiness or magic of their model, but have all of its faults.

√ **J.-B. Greuze, "The Ungrateful Son (A Father's Curse)," (Salon of 1765)**

Imagine a room into which scarcely any light can penetrate except through the door, when it is open, or, when the door is closed, through a square opening above it. Let your eyes wander around this dismal room: they will perceive nothing but poverty. In one corner, however, to the right, there is a bed that does not seem too bad; it has been carefully made. In the foreground, on the same side, is a large, black leather confessional which looks fairly comfortable to sit on: seat the ungrateful son's father upon that. Close to the door, place a low cupboard, and beside the failing old man a small table, on top of which is a bowl of soup that has just been brought to him.

Despite the fact that the eldest son of this family should have been the support of his old father, his mother, and his brothers, he has enlisted. Yet even so, he refuses to leave without having extracted further financial assistance from these wretched and unhappy folk. He has come in with an old soldier; he has made his demands. His father is outraged; he does not mince words with this unnatural child who has forsaken his father, his mother, and his responsibilities, and who is returning insults for his father's reproaches. We see the son in the center of the picture; he has a violent, insolent, angry air; his right arm is raised against his father, over the head of one of his sisters; he is standing very upright, his raised hand expressing a threat; he has his hat on; his gesture and his expression are equally insolent. The good old man, who has loved his children but never permitted any of them to show him disrespect, is making an effort to rise from his chair; but one of his daughters, kneeling in front of him, is clutching the bottom of his coat in an attempt to restrain him. Surrounding the young rake are his eldest sister, his mother, and one of his little brothers. His mother has her arms around his body; he brutally disengages himself and spurns her with his foot. The mother looks crushed and grief-stricken; the eldest sister has also come between her brother and her father; judging by their attitudes, both mother and sister seem to be trying to conceal the two men from each other. The sister has seized her brother by his coat; they way she is pulling at it speaks for itself: "What are you doing, wretch? You are spurning your mother, you are threatening your father. Get down on your knees and beg forgiveness." Meanwhile, with one hand covering his eyes, the little brother is weeping; with his other hand, he is hanging on to his elder brother's arm and trying to drag him out of the house. Behind the old man's chair, the youngest brother of all is standing with a frightened, bewildered look. At the opposite end of the room, near the door, the old soldier who enlisted the son and then came back with him to his parents' home is leaving, his back turned to what is happening, his saber under his arm, his head lowered. And I almost forgot to add that in the foreground, in the midst of all this tumult, there is a dog whose barks add to the uproar.

Everything in this sketch is skillful, well ordered, properly characterized, clear: the grief, even the weakness of the mother for a child she has spoiled; the violence of the old man; the various actions of the sisters and young children; the insolence of the ungrateful son; and the tact of the old soldier, who cannot help but be shocked at what is going on. And the barking dog is an example of Greuze's quite special gift for inventing meaningful details.

J.-B.-S. Chardin (Salon of 1763)

Here is the real painter; here is the true colorist.

There are several small paintings by Chardin at the Salon. Nearly all represent fruits and the accessories of a meal. They are nature itself; the objects seem to come forward from the canvas and have a look of reality which deceives the eye.

The one you see as you walk up the stairs is particularly worth your attention. On top of a table, the artist has placed an old Chinese porcelain vase, two biscuits, a jar of olives, a basket of fruit, two glasses half-filled with wine, a Seville orange, and a meat pie.

When I look at other artists' paintings, I feel I need to make myself a new pair of eyes; to see Chardin's I only need to keep those which nature gave me and use them well.

If I wanted my child to be a painter, this is the painting I should buy. "Copy this," I should say to him, "copy it again." But perhaps nature itself is not more difficult to copy.

For the porcelain vase is truly of porcelain; those olives are really separated from the eye by the water in which they float; you have only to take those biscuits and eat them, to cut and squeeze that orange, to drink that glass of wine, peel those fruits and put the knife to the pie.

Here is the man who truly understands the harmony of colors and reflections. Oh, Chardin! What you mix on your palette is not white, red, or black pigment, but the very substance of things; it is the air and light itself which you take on the tip of your brush and place on the canvas.

After my child had copied and recopied this work, I should set him to work on the same master's *The Gutted Skate*. The subject is repellent, but here is the very flesh of the fish, its skin, its blood—the sight of the thing itself would not affect you otherwise. . . .

This magic is beyond comprehension. There are thick layers of paint, laid one on top of the other, which interpenetrate from the bottom to the top layer. In other places, it is as if a vapor had been breathed on the canvas; in others still, as if a light foam had been thrown on it. Rubens, Berghem, Greuze, Loutherbourg could explain this technique better than I, for all of them could make your eyes feel its effect. Come close, and everything becomes confused, flattens out and vanishes; move back, and everything takes shape once again and recomposes itself.

I have been told that Greuze, on entering the Salon and noticing the painting by Chardin which I have just described, looked at it and walked on, heaving a deep sigh: this eulogy is briefer and better than mine.

Who will pay for Chardin's paintings when this rare man will be no more? And I ought to tell you that this artist possesses excellent common sense and discusses his art marvellously well.

To hell with Apelle's famous Curtain and with Zeuxis' Grapes! It is not difficult to fool an impatient artist, and animals make bad critics of painting. We have seen the birds at the Royal gardens butting their heads against the most badly painted perspectives. But Chardin can deceive you and me whenever he wishes.

From *Essays on Painting* (1766)

Following his review of the Salon of 1765, Diderot wrote Essais sur la peinture *as a demonstration of the theoretical bases of his criticism and as proof of his qualifications as a critic. Cast in the form of letters addressed to Grimm, the* Essais *appeared in the manuscript* Correspondance littéraire *during the last months of 1766. When they were at last published in print, in 1796, Goethe, strongly impressed, drew Schiller's attention to them, and was inspired to write a critique of Diderot's notion of "truth of nature," opposing to it his own idea of a particular "truth of art" ("Diderots Versuch über die Malerei,"* Propylaeen, I, 2, 1799).

Nature does nothing incorrectly. Every form, whether beautiful or ugly, has its cause; and of all creatures in existence there is not one which is not as it necessarily must be.

Look at that woman who lost her eyes in her youth. The eyelids have not been pressed forward by the growth of the eyeball, they have sunk back into the cavity of the eye and become smaller. The upper lids have pulled down the eyebrows, the lower lids have slightly raised the cheeks; the upper lip has been affected by this and has risen. Every part of the face has been altered to some degree, depending on its distance from or nearness to the injured part. But do you think that the face only was affected, and that the neck, the shoulders, the breast were spared? It may seem so to your eyes or mine. But call Nature, show her this neck, these shoulders, this breast, and Nature will say: "This is the neck, these are the shoulders, this is the breast of a woman who lost her eyes when she was young."

We say of a man who passes us in the street that he is badly built. Yes, according to our poor rules, but not according to Nature. We say of a statue that it has the most beautiful proportions. Yes, according to our poor rules, but what about Nature's?

Let me . . . put a veil over the Medici Venus, in such a way as to expose only the tip of her foot. If Nature were called upon to complete the figure, starting from this tip of a foot, you might be surprised to find a hideous, misshapen monster come into being under her pencil. I should be surprised if it were otherwise. . . .

If I were initiated into the mysteries of art, I might know to what extent the artist must submit to conventional rules of proportion, and I would tell you. But this I know, that Nature's despotism overrules them, and that the age and circumstance of the subject force us to modify them in a hundred different ways. I have never heard a figure called badly drawn, when it showed clearly by its outward form the subject's age, habits and aptitudes for performing his daily tasks. For it is these functions which determine the figure's size, and the true proportions of its limbs, taken singly or as a whole. Thus I see before me the child, the grown man, the oldster, the savage, the civilized man, the magistrate, the soldier, and the porter. The hardest thing to draw would be the figure of a man of twenty-five who had suddenly sprung from the ground and done nothing as yet; but that man is a figment of the imagination.

Childhood approaches caricature, and the same could be said for old age. The child is a fluid, shapeless mass trying to develop itself. The old man is also shapeless, but dry and tending to reabsortion and annihilation. It is only in the interval between these two ages, after the onset of manhood and before the end of virility, that the artist submits to the purity and rigorous precision of the form before him, and that a little more or a little less in the conduct of the contour produces or destroys beauty.

But you will tell me: however the age or occupation may alter the form, yet the organs remain. To be sure, and that is why one has to know them, I admit. It is the reason for studying anatomy.

The study of anatomy has its advantages, no doubt, but isn't there a danger that it will stick too much in the artist's mind, that it will make him want to show off his knowledge, that it will lead his eye astray from the outward surface, and that, in spite of skin and flesh, it will make him think only of the muscle, of where it springs from, and how it is fixed and joined. He may dwell on all this too much, become dry and hard, and remind us of his confounded muscle-man even in his female figures. Since I can only show the exterior form, I should prefer to be taught to see it well, and to be spared this vile knowledge which I must forget.

They say that we study anatomy to sharpen our observation of nature; but experience shows that, after studying it, it is hard to see nature as she really is.

. . . Those seven years spent at the Academy, drawing from models, do you think them well spent? Shall I tell you what I think of it? I believe that in these seven cruel, laborious years you learn *mannerisms* in drawing. All those stiff, contrived, academic positions, all those gestures coldly and awkwardly struck by some poor devil, always the same poor devil, paid for coming three times a week to undress and be made to pose by a professor—what does all this have to do with nature, its positions, its gestures? What is there in common between the man who draws water from the well in your yard and the academy model who, without actually pulling the weight, awkwardly simulates this action on a studio platform? What is there in common between the man who pretends to be dying and the one who is really expiring in his bed, or is being knocked down in the street? What likeness is there between the model in a fighting pose and the brawler at the crossroads? These men who seem to plead, pray, sleep, reflect, or faint with care, what have they in common with the peasant struck down by fatigue, the philosopher meditating by the fireplace, or the man fainting in the crush of a mob? Nothing, my friend, nothing.

To cap this absurdity, one might as well send students to study the graces with Marcel or Dupré, or some other dancing master. Meanwhile the truth of nature is forgotten. The artist's imagination is filled with false actions, positions, and figures, contrived, ridiculous and cold. His imagination is stocked with them, and from his imagination they rise to fill his canvases. Every time he takes up his pencil or brush, those wretched phantoms appear before him; he cannot forget them or drive them out of his head. I once knew a young man of excellent taste who, before he would draw a line on canvas, used to kneel and pray: "Lord, deliver me from the model." If nowadays you rarely see a picture containing groups of figures without recognizing those academic figures, actions, or gestures which disgust a man of taste and please only those who are ignorant of truth, you must lay the blame on the constant study of academic models.

You will not learn to understand the general harmony of movements at the Academy, that harmony which can be felt and seen, and which pervades the body from head to foot. If a woman allows her head to droop forward, all the limbs feel the force of its weight; if she lifts it and holds it straight, all the machinery of her body participates in the motion.

Yes, there is a kind of art, a great art, even, in posing the model; you should see how proud the professor is of his work. And never fear that he will ever tell that poor devil of a hireling: "My friend, choose your own position, stand in any posture you like." No, he prefers to put him in some strange attitude, rather than to allow him to take an easy and natural posture, and yet that is exactly what he should let him do.

I have been tempted a hundred times to say to the art students whom I passed on their way to the Louvre, with their portfolios under their arms: "My friends, how many years have you been drawing there? Two years? Well, that is more than enough. Leave that shop of mannerism. Go visit the Carthusian monks; there you will see the real attitudes of devotion and repentance. Today is the eve of a great feast: go to the parish church, walk among the confessionals, and you will see the true attitudes of piety and penitence. Tomorrow, go to the tavern, and you will see the true gesticulations of angry men. Frequent public places, observe what passes in the streets, the gardens, the markets and houses, and you will learn what are the real gestures in the actions of daily life. Just look at those two companions of yours who are quarreling; see how their quarrel prompts them to assume certain attitudes, quite unconsciously. Observe them carefully, and you will pity the teachings you get from your insipid professor and the pantomime of your vapid model. I am sorry for you, my friends, knowing that some day you will have to throw away all these painfully learned falsehoods for the simplicity and truth of Le Sueur. And yet that is what you will have to do if you want to amount to anything.

"Attitudinizing is one thing, action another. Attitudes are petty and false, all actions beautiful and true."

This is how I should want a school of drawing to be conducted: after the student has learned to draw with facility after engravings and casts, I shall make him draw the male and the female model for two years. Then I shall expose him to children and adults, mature men and the aged, models of every age and sex, taken from every layer of society, to all of human nature, in short. If I pay them well, the models will crowd to the door of my academy; in a country which condones slavery, I should make them come. In these various models, the professor will make him observe the irregularities which daily work and the habits of life, of social situation, and of age have produced in the forms of their bodies. My pupil will not see professional models more frequently than once in two weeks, and the professor will leave the choice of the pose to the models themselves. After the drawing session, a skilled anatomist will explain the anatomical structure to my pupil, and make him apply this lesson to the living, moving nude. The student shall not draw cadavers more than twelve times a year. This will suffice to make him realize that flesh over bone is to be drawn unlike flesh not so supported, and that the line in the one case is rounded, angular in the other, and that if he neglects these refinements, the whole will look like an inflated bladder or a ball of cotton.

Strict imitation of nature would do away with mannerisms of drawing and color. Mannerism comes from the teacher, the academy, the school, and even from the Antique.

*   *   *

If taste is a matter of caprice, if there is no principle of beauty, then what is the source of those delightful emotions which arise so suddenly, so involuntarily, so tumultuously from the depths of our souls, which expand or constrict them, and bring tears of joy, sorrow, and admiration to our eyes at the sight of some great moral action? Away with you, Sophist! You will never convince my heart that it should not tremble or my viscera that they should not be moved.

The true, the good, and the beautiful are closely linked. Add to one of the first two qualities some rare and striking circumstance, and the true will be beautiful, and the good will be beautiful. . . .

I see a high mountain, covered with a dark, ancient, deep forest. I see and hear the thunderous cascade of a torrent. Its waters dash against the sharp ridges of a rock. The sun is setting, and it transforms into diamonds the drops which hang from the ragged edges of the stone. Further on, the waters, having overcome the obstacles which hindered them, are gathered into a vast, wide channel which leads them at last toward a mill where under the weight of great mill stones the common food of man is ground. I see the mill, I see its wheels whitened by the foam, and between the willows I catch sight of the roof of the miller's cottage: I withdraw into myself and fall into revery.

Yes, the forest which takes me to the beginning of the world is a beautiful thing; yes, that rock, an image of constancy and duration, is a beautiful thing; yes, these drops scattered by the sun's rays and diffracted into sparkling, liquid diamonds are beautiful; and, certainly, the noise, the thunder of a torrent, which breaks the vast silence and solitude of the mountain and brings a shock, a secret terror to my soul, is beautiful.

But those willows, that cottage, those animals grazing nearby, is not my pleasure increased by the sight of these useful things? And what a difference there is, in this respect, between the ordinary spectator and the philosopher! For his reflective insight sees the forest tree transformed into a ship's mast which will some day be proudly reared against the winds and gales; he sees the crude metal in the depths of the mountain fused in the ardent furnace and cast into the machines which fertilize the earth or kill its inhabitants; he sees in the rocks the stones of which will be built the palaces of kings or the temples of gods. . . .

Thus imagination, sensibility, and knowledge increase our pleasure. Neither nature, nor art which copies her, mean anything to a cold or stupid man; and they mean very little to the ignorant. . . .

Experience and study, these are the preliminary requirements, both for the maker and for the judge of art. And I also require that they possess sensibility. . . .

From *Pensées détachées sur la peinture* (1776–1781)

The Pensées détachées *are a gathering of aphoristic fragments, written for the most part about 1776–1777, with later additions, which Diderot may originally have intended to combine into a systematic treatise. They reflect recent impressions, gained during travels in Holland, Germany, and Russia in 1773–1774 when he visited the galleries of Leyden, Düsseldorf, Dresden, and Saint Petersburg. They also reflect the influence, as Paul Vernière has pointed out,[13] of the German historian and critic, Christian Ludwig von Hagedorn, whose* Betrachtungen über die Malerei *(1762) Diderot had read in translation. From Hagedorn, he took not only anecdotes and learned quotations, but also observations concerning effects of color and of light which corresponded to his own increasing interest in the purely visual qualities of painting.*

Every work of sculpture or painting must be the expression of a great principle, a lesson for the spectator—otherwise it remains mute.

*   *   *

Two qualities essential for the artist: morality and perspective.

*   *   *

13 Denis Diderot, *Oeuvres esthétiques* (ed. Paul Vernière), Paris, Garnier Frères, n.d. (1959), pp. 743 ff.

In every imitation of nature, there is a technical and a moral element. The judgment of the moral element belongs to all men of taste, that of the technical to the artists only.

*   *   *

Whatever the bit of nature you contemplate, be it wild or cultivated, poor or rich, deserted or populous, you will always find in it two enchanting qualities: truth and harmony.

*   *   *

Transport Salvator Rosa to the icy regions near the pole, and his genius will embellish them.

*   *   *

Frighten me, if you will, but let the terror which you inspire in me be tempered by some grand moral idea.

*   *   *

One finds poets among the painters, and painters among the poets. The sight of the paintings of the great masters is as useful to an author as is the reading of great literature to a painter.

*   *   *

A question which is not as ridiculous as it may seem: is it possible to have pure taste, when one's heart is corrupt?

*   *   *

Everything common is simple, but everything simple is not common. Simplicity is one of the chief characteristics of beauty; it is essential to the sublime.

*   *   *

Originality does not exclude simplicity.

*   *   *

One composition is meager, though it has many figures; another is rich, though it has few.

*   *   *

Paint as they spoke in Sparta.

* * *

Talent imitates nature, taste guides choice; nevertheless, I like rusticity better than affectation, and would give ten Watteaus for one Teniers. I prefer Virgil to Fontenelle, and like Theocritus better than both; though he may lack the elegance of the first, he is truer, and free from the affectation of the other.

* * *

I am no Capucin, but I confess that I should gladly sacrifice the pleasure of seeing attractive nudities, if I could hasten the moment when painting and sculpture, having become more decent and moral, will compete with the other arts in inspiring virtue and purifying manners. It seems to me that I have seen enough tits and behinds. These seductive things interfere with the soul's emotions by troubling the senses.

* * *

The moment an artist thinks of money, he loses his feeling for beauty.

* * *

All that has been said about elliptical, circular, serpentine and undulating lines is absurd. Everything has its own line of beauty, and that of the eye is not the same as that of the knee.

And supposing that the undulating line were the human body's line of beauty, among a thousand undulating lines, which is the best?

* * *

Begging Aristotle's pardon, I think it is false criticism to deduce exclusive rules from the most perfect works of art, as if the ways of pleasing were not numberless. There is hardly a rule which genius cannot successfully breach. The band of slaves, to be sure, while admiring, will shout sacrilege.

* * *

It is possible that no one has ever told the pupils of any school that the angle of reflection of light, like that of other bodies, is equal to the angle of incidence.

* * *

Given the point of highest light and the general arrangement of the picture, I imagine a multitude of reflected rays which intercross, and cross the direct light. How does the artist manage to straighten out this confusion? And if he does not care, how can his composition please me?

*   *   *

I arise before the sun. I let my eyes wander over a landscape enlivened by mountains which are clothed in green; great, tufted trees rise from the heights, vast fields spread out below, and these fields are traversed by the windings of a river. Over there stands a castle, here a thatched hut. I see a shepherd approaching from the distance, followed by his flock. He has hardly emerged from the hamlet, and the dust still hides his animals from my sight. All this silent and rather monotonous scene has its peculiar drab and material colors. Meanwhile the sun appears, and everything is suddenly transformed through numberless exchanges of light; it is another picture altogether, in which there remains not a leaf, not a blade of grass, not a dot of the first. Look me in the eye, Vernet, and tell me: are you the sun's rival? can you match this marvel with your brush?

*   *   *

2

Revolution

INTRODUCTION

The Enlightenment generated the energies which brought about its own dissolution. The momentum of reform which it had started increased to a point at which it could no longer be controlled. The reformers found themselves irresistibly drawn into the vortex of revolution by the current of their own ideas. In the arts, this process can be followed in the progressive radicalization of two main strands of thought, both of which had their roots in the philosophy of the Enlightenment: naturalism and idealism, the scientific and the ethical components of this philosophy, which were represented in the arts by the advocates of realism on the one hand and those of classicism on the other. What caused them to become revolutionary was their gradual dissociation from the rational framework of social function and their elevation to the level of absolutes. The documents gathered in the following pages illustrate the development of revolutionary naturalism and of revolutionary classicism, and describe the impact of this development on individuals and institutions.

NATURE AND GENIUS

The view that art is the product of acquired knowledge and skill came under attack, in the middle of the 18th century, from writers who stressed the importance of unconscious drives, inspiration, and interior vision in the making of art. According to them, the true work of art is not a construction, but an original creation. The artist, driven by inner necessity, creates as the tree bears fruit, ignorant of rules, indifferent to society. The vital power which acts through him does not imitate nature, it belongs to nature itself, it is natural genius, *and its works have the qualities which are found in nature's authentic creation—organic unity and life.*

An early expression of this quasi-biological conception of creative art occurs in Edward Young's Conjectures on Original Composition *(1759):*

An Original may be said to be of *vegetable* nature; it rises spontaneously from the vital root of genius; it *grows,* it is not *made;* Imitations are often a sort of *manufacture,* wrought up by those *mechanics,* art and *labour,* out of pre-existent materials not their own. . . . Modern writers have a *choice* to make

. . . they may soar in the regions of *liberty,* or move in the soft fetters of easy *imitation.*[14]

The living plant came to be a favorite image for the expression of this conception of art, just as the well-functioning machine had been an emblem of the Enlightenment. A special beauty began to be discovered in those forms of nature or of art which, though lacking regularity and smoothness, possessed the vigor and character expressive of organic growth. Shakespeare and Gothic architecture profited from this change in taste. Some writers advanced the view that art was not a product of cultural development, but of human nature itself, and therefore more likely to be found in the naïve, primitive, "natural" man than in the creature of polished society. What had begun as a critique of the excesses of the Enlightenment gradually turned into an attack on culture itself. The widespread recoil from overcivilization had its most influential spokesman in J. J. Rousseau who introduced a treatise on education (Émile, 1762) with the lament:

Everything is good as it comes from the hands of the Author of Nature; everything degenerates in the hands of man. He forces one country to nourish the productions of another; one tree to bear the fruits of another. He mingles and confounds the climates, the elements, the seasons; he mutilates his dog, his horse, his slave; he overturns everything, disfigures everything; he loves deformity and monsters; he will have nothing as Nature made it, not even man; man must be trained for man's service; he must be shaped to suit his fashion, like a tree in his garden.[15]

In Germany, English notions of vegetable creation and Rousseau's idea of primitive virtue became combined in a theory of historical and cultural evolution. J. G. Herder studied the growth of language, literature and art as the characteristic expression of national genius. Other German writers of the decades between 1770 and 1790 carried the new naturalism to its anarchical extreme. The ironic nickname of "Storm and Stress" (from the German Sturm und Drang) *has come to be applied to them in particular, but it fits equally well many of their contemporaries in England and France, young poets and artists who claimed the freedom to express their impulses and intuitions, contemptuous of polite manners and refinements, hostile to rules and even to reason itself. The international movement of radical naturalism which Storm and Stress exemplified was, in fact, romanticism in the earliest of its various shapes.*

Johann Wolfgang Goethe (1749–1832)

As a youth, Goethe had wavered between art and poetry. In his student years in Leipzig, he took lessons from the painter Oeser who,

[14] M. W. Steinke, *Edward Young's "Conjectures on Original Composition" in England and Germany*, New York, 1917, pp. 45–47.

[15] J. J. Rousseau, *Émile, ou de l'éducation*, Paris, Firmin-Didot, 1851, p. 1.

fifteen years before, had been Winckelmann's artistic mentor. He continued throughout his later life to think and to express himself in terms of visual experience, and to consider aesthetic questions from the point of view of the artist, rather than that of the poet.

Goethe arrived in Strassburg in 1770, in his twenty-first year. The immense cathedral rising from among narrow lanes made on him "a most peculiar impression, which stayed with me, obscurely, since I was for the time being unable to account for it." This first shock of surprise and the subsequent falling away of his prejudices against the "barbarian" Gothic were the personal experiences which eventually led him to write the essay On German Architecture—D. M. Ervini a Steinbach, 1773. *It is noteworthy that Goethe received the stimulus for this tribute to German tradition, to native genius, and to national art on the soil of France, then the mainstay of cosmopolitan culture and center of the Enlightenment. The dominant intellectual influence on him during his sojourn in Strassburg was Johann Gottfried Herder (1744–1803), one of the leaders of the Storm and Stress. Herder directed Goethe's interest to national poetry, to folk song and myth, and to transcendent genius, as personified by Shakespeare. Herder's* On the Origins of Language *(1772) was probably in Goethe's mind when he wrote the essay on German architecture, but his ostensible aim was to take issue with a much older book, the Abbé Laugier's* Observations sur l'architecture *(1753). His choice of this antagonist seems odd: the Abbé's cautious appreciation of the Gothic may actually have helped Goethe to crystallize his own thoughts; Laugier's comparison of Gothic forms with the forms of plant life, at any rate, anticipated Goethe's rather similar interpretation. But these affinities remained unacknowledged in the essay. Goethe, needing the Frenchman as an adversary, sharply debated his theory of the origin of architecture and his insistence on the importance of the column as an original and essential architectural element. The middle section of the essay, which contains Goethe's attack on Laugier's neoclassical notions, has been largely omitted from the translation which follows, because it does not actually bear on the real theme. Goethe's deeper intention in writing his tribute to Erwin von Steinbach was not, after all, to offer an historical or technical appraisal of the Gothic, but to issue a manifesto about creative genius, and about the organic unity and national character of art. His main assertions concerned the parallel between artistic creation and organic growth, one of the guiding ideas of Storm and Stress. The cathedral tower seemed to him a tree, a work of genius, and hence of nature, rather than an artificial composition. And the genius through whom nature had worked in creating the Gothic tower was German: the characteristic Gothic form, Goethe erroneously thought, derived from a national, German source, and was therefore beyond the comprehension of the French critic.*

Goethe later omitted this youthful article from the body of his collected works, and revised or repudiated most of the ideas which it expressed; but these ideas were to be taken up again by later generations and to exert a shaping influence on the beginnings of romantic art theory and art history. The passionate tone of the essay, and its rough, abrupt, untrammeled style—a torment to the translator—are themselves manifestations of turbulent genius and a document of the emotional climate of Storm and Stress.[16]

From *On German Architecture—D. M. Ervini a Steinbach, 1773*

When, dear Erwin, I walked on your grave, looking for the stone which would tell me ANNO DOMINI 1318, XVI. KAL. FEBR. OBIIT MAGISTER ERVINIUS, GUBERNATOR FABRICIAE ECCLESIAE ARGENTINENSIS, so that I might pour out my veneration for you at this holy place, I could not find it, and none of your compatriots could show it to me. My soul was deeply saddened, and my heart—younger, warmer, more foolish, and better than now—promised you a monument in marble or sandstone, whatever I might be able to afford, when I should come into the quiet enjoyment of my possessions.

But what use monuments! you have built the most magnificent of all to yourself, and if the ants which crawl around it do not care for your name, this is a fate which you share with the Architect who raised mountains into the clouds.

Few men have conceived a Babel-thought in their soul, whole, grand, and compellingly beautiful down to its smallest parts, like God's trees. Fewer still have met with a thousand willing hands to excavate the rock and conjure up steep heights, and have been able at their death to tell their sons: "I shall stay with you in the works of my spirit; carry this beginning on into the clouds."

What need do you have of a monument! and from me! When the mob uses holy names, it is superstition or blasphemy. At the sight of your colossus, sickly dilettantes will suffer fits of vertigo, but strong souls will understand you without an interpreter.

Therefore, excellent man! before I launch my little patched-up boat onto the Ocean once again, more likely to meet with death than fortune, I shall carve your name into a beech as slender as your tower, here in this grove verdant with the names of my loves. And I shall suspend by its four corners this handkerchief full of gifts, not unlike that cloth filled with clean and unclean beasts which was lowered from the clouds to the Apostle. These flowers, blossoms, leaves, dry grass and moss,

---

[16] Translated, with minor omissions, from *Goethes Werke* (Sophien Ausgabe), Weimar, 1896, I. Abtheilung, XXXVII, 137 ff.

and mushrooms sprung up overnight, gathered for my botanical diversion on a walk through plain country, I shall now let rot in your honor.

"It is in petty taste," says the Italian, passing by. "Childishness," drawls the Frenchman and triumphantly drums on his neoclassical snuff-box. But what gives you the right to scorn?

Didn't the genius of Antiquity, rising from its grave, enslave your spirit, Dago? Crawling through mighty ruins to beg their proportions, you patched together villas from sacred fragments, and now consider yourself the guardian of art's secrets, because you can explain gigantic buildings inch by inch. Had you given way to feeling, rather than measurements, you would have been touched by the spirit of the mighty piles at which you gaped. Then you would not merely have imitated what the Ancients did, and did beautifully, your own designs would have become compelling and true, and living beauty would have sprung from them.

Instead, you gave to your want a coating of seeming truth and beauty. You were impressed by the magnificent effect of columns, you wanted to use columns, too, and you walled them in. You also wanted columns standing in rows, and you encircled the forecourt of St. Peter's with marble porticos which lead nowhere. And Mother Nature, who hates and despises everything inappropriate and unnecessary, made your rabble prostitute this magnificence by using it as a public sewer, so that you must avert your eyes and hold your nose when passing this marvel.

The world goes on: the artist's whim serves the egoism of the rich; travel writers gape, and our wits or so-called philosophers spin principles and histories of art from flimsy fairy tales, while real men are murdered by the demon in the forecourt of art's sanctuary.

Principles hurt genius more than examples. Individual men before him may have worked out the particular details, but from his soul these parts first spring, grown into one eternal whole. Schools and principles, by contrast, paralyze our powers of insight and action. . . .

Our houses . . . are formed by four walls on four sides . . . they are made up of surfaces which, the wider they spread and the more boldly they rise, depress our spirit with their unbearable monotony. But fortunately the genius who inspired Erwin von Steinbach comes to our rescue: "Enrich and animate the immense wall which you shall raise to the sky, let it rise like a lofty, wide-spreading tree of God, declaring with a thousand branches, a million twigs, and with leaves numerous as the sands of the sea, the glory of the Lord, its Master."

When I first went to the cathedral, my head was filled with general notions of taste. I honored by hearsay the principles of the harmony of masses and purity of forms, and was the declared enemy of the confused capriciousness of Gothic ornament. Under the heading of Gothic, as in a dictionary article, I had compiled all the synonymous misunderstandings concerning the ill-defined, the disordered, unnatural, pieced-to-gether, patched-up, and overladen which had ever passed through my mind. No wiser than a people which calls "barbaric" all the world it does not know, I called *gothic* whatever did not fit my system. I made no distinction between the contorted, painted puppets and decorations with which our noble bourgeois fancify their houses and the awesome relics of our older German architecture. Certain bizarre curlicues in them made me join the common cry of "Smothered in ornament!" and I shuddered as I went to look at the misshapen, bristling monster.

What unexpected emotions overcame me at the sight of the cathedral, when finally I stood before it! One impression, whole and grand, filled my soul, an impression which, resulting from the harmony of a thousand separate parts, I could savor and enjoy, but neither explain nor understand. They say that such are the joys of heaven. And I returned often, to taste these heavenly-earthly pleasures, and to embrace the gigantic spirit of our elder brothers in their works. How often have I gone back to contemplate this dignity and magnificence from every side, at every distance, and in every kind of light. It is burdensome to a man's mind to find the work of his brother so exalted that he must bow and worship before it. How often has the friendly, calming twilight soothed my eyes, worn out from too much looking; for in the twilight the countless parts melted into one great mass which confronted my soul in grandiose simplicity and gloriously set free my powers of enjoyment and comprehension. It was then that the genius of the great builder became revealed to me in subtle intuitions. "Why are you surprised," he whispered to me, "all these masses were necessary. Don't you also find them in all the earlier churches of my town? I have merely brought their arbitrary dimensions into harmonious proportions. See how, above the main portal which dominates the two lesser ones, the wide circle of the window opens, corresponding to the nave of the church, when it might have been merely an opening to let in the daylight. See how, high above, the belfry demands smaller windows! All this was necessary, and I gave it beautiful form. But oh! when I float through the dark, steep openings at this side which seem vacant and useless—into their soaring forms I put the secret power which was to have lifted into the sky the two towers of which only one, alas, now stands, sadly, without the five-peaked crown which I meant to give it, so that the surrounding provinces might pay homage to it and to its royal brother!" And so he left me, and I sank into sympathetic sadness, until the birds of morning which nest in the tower's thousand openings joyfully greeted the sun and roused me from my sleep. How fresh the tower shone in the light of the fragment morning! How joyfully I reached out toward it, seeing its grand harmonious mass alive in its countless parts: everything formed, down to the smallest fiber, everything serving the whole, as in works of eternal nature, the massive, immense structure rising lightly skyward; everything about it diaphanous, yet built for eternity. I owe it to your teaching, genius! that I no longer feel dizzy at your depth, and that into my soul has fallen a drop of the joyful quiet of the spirit who can contemplate a creation such as this and say, God-like: "It is good."

No wonder it makes me angry, divine Erwin, when a German art scholar, misled by envious neighbors, ignores his own advantage and belittles your work with the misunderstood term "Gothic." He should rather thank God that he can declare: this is German architecture, seeing that the Italian cannot boast of an architecture of his own, and the Frenchman even less. And if you will not grant our nation its priority, try to prove that the Goths really did build like this—you won't find it easy. In the end, if you cannot show that there was a Homer before Homer, we shall gladly let you tell the story of petty successes and failures, and go on worshipping before the work of the master in whose creation the scattered elements were first joined into one living whole. And you, our dear brother in the search after truth and beauty, close your ears to all the verbiage about art: come, enjoy and look. Take care not to desecrate the name of your noblest artist, and hurry to behold his excellent work. If it gives you a disagreeable impression, or none at all, then good-bye to you, let the horses be hitched, and off to Paris!

But let me join with you, dear fellow, standing there deeply moved, trying to resolve a conflict in your soul, feeling at one moment the irresistible power of this great whole, and calling me a dreamer the next for seeing beauty where you only see power and rough vigor. Don't let a misunderstanding separate us, don't let the effeminate doctrine of modern aesthetics spoil you for the meaningful and rugged, lest you acquire a sickly taste for the insignificant and smooth. They want you to believe that the arts owe their beginning to our supposed urge to beautify our surroundings. That is not true! or strictly holds true only for burghers and artisans, not for philosophers.

Art is creative long before it becomes beautiful, and yet is truly great art, truer and greater, in fact, than the beautiful. For there is a creative nature in man which becomes active as soon as his existence is assured. When he has no cares or fears, the Demigod, productive in his repose, reaches out for matter into which to breathe his spirit. The savage transforms coconuts, feathers, and even his own body into weird images, strange-featured and high-colored. And though his work will consist of the most arbitrary forms, it will be coherent, despite its lack of proportion, because one sensibility shaped it into a characteristic whole.

This art of the characteristic is the only true art. Whatever it produces, prompted by intense, individual, and original feeling, careless or oblivious of everything foreign to it, has wholeness and vitality. It does not matter whether it was begot by rude savagery or civilized sensibility. You will find it in innumerable gradations among nations and individuals. The higher the soul rises toward an awareness of the proportions which alone are beautiful and eternal, whose main accords can be demonstrated but whose secrets can only be felt and in which the God-like, vital genius bathes in blissful harmony, the more these beauties enter into the spirit and seem to become one with it, so that it will not be satisfied by anything else nor create anything else, the more happy and magnificent is the artist, and the more deeply we bow before him, worshipping him as the anointed of God.

No one can topple Erwin from his eminence. Here is his work: approach it and discover the deepest feelings of truth and beauty of proportions, sprung from a plain and vigorous German soul, alive in the confinement of the dark, priest-ridden Middle Ages.

But what about our own age? It has renounced its genius and sent out its sons to gather foreign plants which will be their ruin. The frivolous Frenchman, an even worse pilferer, at least has the wit of giving his loot some appearance of unity. He is currently busy building a marvellous temple for his St. Magdalen with Greek columns and German vaults. And I have seen one of our artists who had been commissioned to design a portal for an old German church produce the model of a stately antique colonnade.

I don't want to harp on my hatred for our painters of cosmetic dolls. They have caught the eye of our women with their theatrical poses, lying complexions, and garish clothes. Upright Albrecht Dürer, mocked by the novices, I much prefer your most wood-cut figure.

But even you, men of high excellence, who have received the gift of enjoying the highest beauty and who now descend to proclaim your blessedness, even you are harmful to genius. For genius does not want to be uplifted and carried away on the wings of any other, not even on those of Dawn itself. His own powers which first unfolded in the child's dream and were exercised in adolescence send him forth, strong and agile like a mountain lion on the prowl. That is why he is usually trained by Nature: the pedagogues cannot give him the scope which he needs, to act and to enjoy in accordance with his present strength.

Hail to you, Youth, born with a keen eye for proportion, adept at seizing every shape. When one by one the joys of life awaken round you and you feel the ecstatic delight which comes after labor, fear, and hope, like the vintner's lusty shout when the autumn's abundance fills his vessels, like the lively dance of the mower after he has stuck the idle sickle into the roofbeam; when the powerful impulse of desire and suffering animates your brush with greater vigor; when you have striven, suffered, and enjoyed enough, and had your fill of earthly beauty, and have earned your rest in the arms of the goddess, and are worthy to experience in her bosom what gave a new birth to the divine Hercules—then receive him, Heavenly Beauty, mediator between gods and men, so that, greater than Prometheus, he may bring the bliss of the gods down to earth.

Wilhelm Heinse (1746–1803)

A representative of the generation of Storm and Stress, like the young Goethe, his contemporary and friend, Heinse embodied the survival of Baroque attitudes into the period of Neoclassicism. His Letters *from the Düsseldorf Gallery (1776–77) recall in feeling and language Goethe's slightly earlier praise of the Cathedral of Strassburg (see page 72). Both Heinse and Goethe celebrated the creative power of genius, both responded to the energetic and vital in art, both saw in art the manifestation of a life-force comparable to that which acts in nature. But while Goethe found the prototype of creative genius in the shadowy figure of the medieval builder, Erwin von Steinbach, Heinse found it in the much more concrete, historical personality of Rubens, of whose paintings his* Letters *give splendidly colored and animated descriptions. His strong sensuality responded most keenly to the sight of the naked body. In this he recalls Winckelmann, but, unlike Winckelmann, he did not think it necessary to idealize physical beauty; actual sight, touch, and taste were enough for him. His bent was wholly antiphilosophical and untheoretical. Beauty to him was no remote perfection, but a direct sensation deeply relished: "on the tongue clear Hochheimer of '66 vintage, and for the love-warmed fingertips the breast of a young Circassian girl."* [17]

Excerpts from the *Diaries*

Winckelmann and that sterile crowd speak like men possessed, like madmen, when they say that one ought to study and imitate only the Ancients. Actually, what they believe to be their chief goal is merely an easy trick for finding a few natural beauties. They paint and draw only in the midst of plaster phantoms—what nonsense! As if the beauties

[17] The translations from the diaries and letters of Heinse are based on J. J. W. Heinse, *Sämmtliche Werke*, Leipzig, Insel, 1903–1925. The diary excerpts are taken from VIII, Part I, 386, 493, 536, and 555 of this publication; the excerpts from the letters from IX, 338 and 345. For the translations from *Ardinghello*, I have used the edition by Heinrich Laube, published in Leipzig in 1839. The translated passages will be found on pp. 14, 36, 254, 259, 262, and 274 of that edition.

which are in the Apollo, the Laocoon, and the Medici Venus were not around us all the time. Simpletons! Nature is rich and inexhaustible. We are surfeited with the things which the Greek masters saw and recorded in their art, we want something different. Bury yourselves in your hellish emptiness, gnaw and nibble enviously on your Greek models until you die; let's be rid of you, nasty vermin!

The joys and pleasures of superior men decide questions of art, not the pedantry of school masters. Where is the proof that this statue or that sets the rule of art? Nature is the norm which governs this or that statue, and nature is manifold and has many kinds of perfection, you dreary monomaniacs! And yet arms and legs won't become monstrous, and everything in nature will retain its proper proportions.

This is the reason why men of profound mind, when looking at pictures, often have thoughts which never crossed the mind of the poor, drudging painter.

*   *   *

Every form is individual, there exists none which is abstract. It is impossible to imagine the purely ideal figure of a man or woman, infant or old man. A young Aspasia, Phryne or Lais can be raised to a Venus, Diana or Athena . . . but an abstract, merely perfect woman, unaffected by climate or culture, is no more than a phantom, worse even than the fictitious heroine of a novel who at least must speak some particular language and use words which can be understood. And those unbearably empty faces and figures are called high and true art by wretches who have learned their trade with the aid of plaster casts and now look down with contempt on those more vigorous men who carry their own century's beauty in their living hearts.

*   *   *

I do not know whether the Laocoon group is really as beautiful as they say. The more I look at it, the more artificial and choreographic it seems to me. The snakes appear to have been trained, one of them to creep down through the arms, the other to crawl up between the legs, weaving the father and his two little sons into a marble fan. And so that this fan might have a handle, Daddy has been propped up on an altar. I can't find all that extravagant sublimity in his face, and in the faces of the two boys I see grimacing, rather than natural expression.

*   *   *

In the arts, one must early form the habit of seeing no more than what is actually present. This habit is harder to acquire than one might think, but without it one cannot become a good judge. This is why our phantasists, young and old, read marvels into a vignette, though it usually doesn't contain one bit of its supposed meaning. This, too, is why any mediocre statue of Apollo reminded Winckelmann of everything he had read about the god in Homer, Pindar, and Junius, and made him gush dithyrambic praise so as to give fools the goose-bumps. We should try to treat painting and sculpture as objects, not merely as signs.

Letters from the Düsseldorf Gallery (1776–1777)

There once was a man who, under the most fortunate constellation of sun and moon, wind and weather, made the wonderful and mysterious leap from chaos into being. And when he had arrived, in fresh strength, Mother Night cared for him like a tender woman.

And he was born, and grew.

The light of the rising day gradually illuminated his senses. And he held on to every good thing near him, one after the other, with the love and warmth a groom feels for his bride. Thus he won all who were near him and made them his own. He grew into boyhood and adolescence, and his nature became richer.

He possessed too much to keep all; he had to give away part of his self, to his girls and friends, and to their girls and friends, and to others living in undeserved neglect, having received few of God's gifts.

And how did he do it?

Not through words. For words seemed to him too much taken from the surfaces of things, too much made up for humdrum relationships, too generalized, worn and crippled, and of such old usage that most of us mechanically memorize them and carry them with us as dead capital, not knowing where we got them. He felt that the finest fruits of his mind when mouthed turned into empty husks, into monotony, and he lost all desire to make use of this means. Instead, he chose another, more joyful way of rendering every thing in its full individuality, namely the magic of pictorial illusion, the most natural among the arts and—after sculpture, which is too confining—the first and noblest. He learned the language of day and night, of color, light and shadow; he already knew the line of life. He then tried the distant and ideal, borrowed from school masters who knew their grammar sufficiently well, and tried his hand at doing dogs and cats, girls, boys, birds and trees, keeping busy at all hours.

After he had mastered this, he went to study in the great school of Italy. He read and studied the works of the Greeks of two thousand years ago which he found in Venice, in Florence, and in Rome, Queen-Mother of the World. He copied the most beautiful of them, and sang Buonarotti's odes and Caravaggio's folk songs; then studied the works of Titian and his predecessors, listened to the excellent comedies and tragedies, the bucolic plays and operas staged by the great Italian masters, and relished their epics.

For seven years, he carried on in this way, making acquaintances and friends among various noblemen, giving lessons, lecturing, and composing a song full of life and strength. Then he went home, with a bag full of money and with many other precious things besides.

Here he made himself comfortable again, rested, slept, and went about among his own dear relatives, their rooms, cloisters, and fields, among the meadows and willows, in the horse stables, among hills, forests and valleys, groves and plains, near brooks and lakes, a man so dear, so good and loyal, and endowed with such gifts of fortune and mind that he could not fail to become the favorite of his people. He spoke only the language of his natural self, using it with the mastery and insight with which Homer and Aristophanes had spoken theirs. His fame spread to all countries.

And the name of this man is *Rubens*. . . .

*   *   *

The Flight of the Amazons.   A terrible battle of the sexes, to be savored fully only by those who have explored nature's remoter aspects.

A picturesque melee; the victory has finally been decided. The luckless heroines must yield to overwhelming force, they are beaten, and the enemy pursue them across the bridge. The rear guard, perhaps the bravest of all, are taken prisoners or are being furiously slaughtered, but some turn back and slaughter their pursuers. It is a scene of war's delight, made to gladden the heart of a hero: lust after sweat and danger, and with girls who dare to attack men with swords, who are wild, cruel, and yet charming rebels against nature's law. A rare and fearfully beautiful spectacle. At the left of the painting, the scene begins with a distant rush of escaping women and horses. Two brown battle chargers follow, leaping riderless from the bridge. The first so shy and wild that, with its mane fluttering in the wind, it grits its teeth and breathes steam from its nostrils; the other bolts, maddened by the battle. Behind them an Amazon who holds in both hands the head of a general whom she has decapitated on the bridge. His rump still lies there, bleeding into the water . . . The picture is a work of heroic power, recalling Theseus' time: nothing in it is overloaded, every illusion is achieved which colors can accomplish. Power in male shoulders, in arms and fists grasping murderous weapons, in chests and knees, in the rearing, the leap and rush of horses. Looks of fire and heat of pursuit, fury and desperate revenge in flight; highest female courage: hacking, stabbing, tearing down . . . intensest life in the confusion of battle, in the baleful light of a broken morning sky.

The Amazons' flesh is not inert; their bodies are steeled, noble, full of strength and fire. Befitting the Circassian climate and antique usage, they are lightly dressed in an undergarment and a small red mantle draped from the left shoulder which, as they fall into the water, generally drops away, its straps broken or cut, revealing everywhere the motion of beautiful limbs. . . .

From *Ardinghello, or the Happy Isles* (1787)

Heinse's Ardinghello *was one of the first novels to have an artist as its hero and to be centered on questions of art. Its setting is Italy of the late Renaissance and its plot a jumble of swordplay and erotic adventure, interrupted from time to time by passionate discussions of painting or sculpture. The story concludes with the departure of the surviving characters, male and female, for the happy isles of Paros and Naxos, where they will live in beauty, nudity, and sexual freedom.* Ardinghello *is an extraordinary blend of picturesque history and Utopian vision, into which are woven descriptions of Titian's* Venus of Urbino, *of Raphael's frescoes in the Vatican, of the* Laocoon, *the* Medici Venus, *and many other works of classical or Renaissance art which had impressed Heinse during his Italian voyage of 1781–1783. The anarchical, amoral, biased attitudes which the book expresses strike the modern reader as "romantic," compared to the writings of Diderot, for example. But it is also apparent that Heinse's taste in art is much closer to that of Reynolds than that of Blake (see page 150), and that an unfathomable gulf separates him from the piety and sentiment of Wackenroder's* Art-Loving Friar, *that archromantic manifesto, which appeared only ten years after his book (see Vol. II, p. 19).*

[Ardinghello speaks:] I am a Florentine painter, and I am staying here [in Venice] to glory in Venetian flesh, having had too much of Tuscan skeletons. Titian commands the essential part of painting without which all the rest is nothing. There are other things in painting, to be sure, but they are unwholesome and sickly—no matter whether you think them heavenly and excellent, or merely deceitful trickery. To be a really great painter, one must work like Titian. Common opinion decides in this matter, not the opinion of artists. Titian sways all who are not themselves painters, and he even sways the painters when it comes to the main business of painting—which is truth of color, just as drawing is the main point of drawing. Painting is painting, drawing is drawing. Painting cannot exist without truth of color, it could more easily do without design.

The painter concerns himself with surfaces, and these are revealed by color. The essential qualities of the object as such mean much less to him. . . . Drawing is only a necessary evil, proportions are easily determined: color is the goal, the beginning and end of art. Obviously, I am only speaking of the material aspects. It would be ridiculous to value the scaffolding more than the building, or to prefer drawing, an invention of human frailty, to the substance. The hollow and the round, the dark and the light, the hard and the soft, the young and the old—how are they to be expressed if not through color? Form and expression cannot exist without it. The sharpest, most severe lines of Michelangelo are mere dream and shadow compared to the noble life in a head by Titian.

*   *   *

Among the Greeks and Romans, the temple was usually destined for only one of their many gods. It was a dwelling, made to serve him when he came down from Olympus to visit the region, like a king travelling from his residence to some provincial castle. The temple's dimensions, therefore, were not large, and the columns were proportioned accordingly. Every citizen sacrificed individually, and on feast days only the priests and priestesses entered, while the people stood outside. . . .

Our churches, by contrast, are places of assembly in which all the inhabitants of a town will often stay for hours on end. A solemn Gothic cathedral, designed by intelligent barbarians, contains immense open spaces in which the voice of the priest becomes thunder and the people's chant a sea-storm, praising the Father of the Universe and shaking the boldest unbeliever, while the organ, the tyrant of music, roars like a hurricane plowing deep seas. To a man of sound feeling, such a cathedral will put the Greek temple, that mere enlargement of a petty dwelling, to shame—yes, even the loveliest Venus temple by the most tasteful Athenian.

*   *   *

The best subjects for artists, surely, are animals and plants, grasses and trees; these they can represent, but human beings they ought to leave to poets. Landscape will in time replace all other kinds of painting. And thus it will become possible to surpass the Greeks—by treating subjects which they missed.

Men are never impressed by inert matter; all lack of motion suggests death.

*   *   *

All art which is merely pictorial sooner or later makes its lover and possessor suffer the torments of Tantalus. The most beautiful image, even a Praxitelean Venus, eventually turns into a lifeless shadow. It does not stir or move, and therefore returns to the dead stone or the oil and pigment from which it was made. Strongly vital human beings are the first to sense this. I believe that, if the golden age of the Greeks had lasted longer, they would have ended up by throwing their statues into the sea, to rid themselves once for all of this deadness and immobility.

*   *   *

To render life in its full intensity is the most difficult task for all the arts, the pictorial as well as the poetical and musical: storm in nature, murder between man and man, soul-union between man and woman, or the separation and loneliness of loving souls. Mere industry is capable of representing the inanimate; only greatness can render life. Those who were not illuminated by the torch of divinity at the start of their existence will achieve neither a work of high art, nor a sublime action. Beauty is life in form and in movement. Nothing is beautiful which is lifeless or unrelated to life.

Why is the *Torso*, why are the *Horse-Tamers* of Monte Cavallo, why is our *Venus* beautiful? Because they show the highest perfection of human force in the happy enjoyment of its existence. Why *Apollo*, why the *Gladiator?* Because their life is shown effectively at the apex of its power. Why *Laocoon*, why *Niobe?* Because they, too, embody a splendid life, succumbing to stronger power. The poet suggests it with words, the artist gives the very surface of living reality.

*   *   *

The sun had splendidly set, leaving behind it a most beautiful red sky. "If I were a landscape painter," cried Demetrius, "I should paint nothing but skies for a whole year, especially sunsets. What magic, what infinite melodies of light and dark, of cloud-shapes and serene blue! It is nature's poetry. Mountains, palaces, castles, pleasure groves, constant fireworks of light beams, shapes of giants, war and strife, alternating with ever new delights, as the orb of day sinks amidst blazing fires."

Johann Kaspar Lavater (1741–1801)

The Swiss "physiognomist" Lavater taught that character could be read in the formations of face, body, and handwriting. His science was an attempt to give practical application to the pan-naturalism and vitalism of Storm and Stress. Lavater's Physiognomical Fragments for the Promotion of the Knowledge and Love of Mankind *(1775–1778, 1802), from which the following excerpts are taken, went through numerous editions in the original German, and in French and English translations; it was one of the most influential books of its time. Though not primarily concerned with matters of art, Lavater's essays had a special interest for artists, since they dealt with the interpretation of visual appearance and were based on pictorial evidence. The physical body of man and the work of the artist were, according to Lavater, extensions of the creative personality and derived ultimately from the same vital energies. Thus the shape of a nose, the slant of a line of writing, or the style of a painting possessed individual, expressive character and offered themselves to the same kind of diagnostic interpretation.*[18]

From *Physiognomical Fragments* (1775–1802)

On the Congruity of the Human Form

In organization, nature continually acts from within to without, from the center to the circumference. The same vital power that makes the heart beat gives the finger motion: that which roofs the skull arches the finger nail. Art is at variance with itself; not so nature. Her creation is progressive. From the head to the back, from the shoulder to the arm, from the arm to the hand, from the hand to the finger, from the root to the stem, the stem to the branch, the branch to the twig, the twig to the blossom and fruit, each depends on the other, and all on the root; each is similar in nature and in form. No apple of one branch can, with all its properties, be the apple of another; not to say of another tree. . . . Each part of an organized body is an image of the whole, has the character of the whole. The blood in the extremity of the finger has the character of the blood in the heart. The same congeniality is found

---

[18] The passage on the "Congruity of the Human Form" is taken from Thomas Holcroft's translation of Johann Kaspar Lavater, *Essays on Physiognomy* (8th edition), London, 1853, p. 179; the passage on "Genius" from the German text as given in J. C. Lavater's *Physiognomik*, new edition, Vienna, 1829, IV, 82 ff.

in the nerves, in the bones. One spirit lives in all. Each member of the body is in proportion to that whole of which it is a part. . . . One form, one mind, one root, appertain to all. Therefore is each organized body so much a whole that, without discord, destruction, or deformity, nothing can be added or diminished. Everything in man is progressive; everything congenial; form, stature, complexion, hair, skin, veins, nerves, bones, voice, walk, manner, style, passion, love, hatred. One and the same spirit is manifest in all. . . .

   Nature makes no emendations, she labors from one to all. Hers is not disjointed organization; not mosaic work. The more of the mosaic there is in the works of artists, orators, or poets, the less are they natural; the less do they resemble the copious streams of the fountain; the stem extending itself to the remotest branch. . . .

   The human body is a plant; each part has the character of the stem. Suffer me to repeat this continually, since this most evident of all things is continually controverted, among all ranks of men, in words, deeds, books, and works of art.

   It is therefore that I find the greatest incongruities in the heads of the greatest masters. I know no painter of whom I can say he has thoroughly studied the harmony of the human outline, not even Poussin; no, not even Raphael himself. Let anyone class the forms of their countenances, and compare them with the forms of nature; let him for instance draw the outlines of their foreheads, and endeavor to find similar outlines in nature, and he will find incongruities which could not have been expected in such great masters.

Genius

   What is genius? . . . Where there is effectiveness, power, action, thought and feeling which cannot be learned or taught, there is genius, the most apparent and least describable thing, felt but unspoken, like love!

   The characteristic of genius and of all its creations is, in my opinion, *apparition* . . . like the apparition of an angel, it comes not, but is suddenly present, leaves not, but is gone. Like the apparition of an angel, it moves us to the marrow; its immortality rouses the immortality in us; it vanishes, but continues to act after it is gone, leaving us in sweet trembling, in tears of fright, and the pallor of joy. . . . Call it fertility of mind . . . call it elasticity of the soul or senses, and of the nervous system which, alert to all impressions, reacts to them with a rapid charge of vital individuality; call it inherent, natural energy of soul, call it creative power. . . . That which has not been learned or borrowed, which cannot be learned or borrowed, the intimately individual, the inimitable, the divine is genius, the inspired is genius, and is called genius by all nations, in all periods, and will be called thus so long as men think, feel, and speak. Genius flashes, genius creates, it does not contrive, it creates! just as it cannot be contrived, but simply *exists*. . . . Inimitability is the characteristic of genius. Instantaneity, revelation, apparition, *being:* a gift not of man, but of God or Satan.

Henry Fuseli (1741–1825)

Fuseli's early years were spent among the leaders of the movement of Storm and Stress; he knew both Lavater and Goethe. In 1764, he went to England, where he lived by his pen and made himself known as the translator of Winckelmann and Lavater (see pages 5, 86). With Sir Joshua Reynolds' encouragement, he resolved to become an artist, entrusting his education to his own genius and to the inspiring example of Michelangelo. During a long stay in Italy, in 1770–1778, he gained a thorough knowledge of the history of art which, added to his vast literary erudition and command of many languages, made him the most learned artist of his time. He returned to London in 1779 where he remained, until the end of his long life, an exotic but respected figure in the world of art, holding the positions of professor and keeper of the Royal Academy. He managed to be on good terms with both the academicians and the Academy's archenemy, William Blake, who wrote of him:

> The only Man that e'er I knew
> Who did not make me almost spew
> Was Fuseli: he was both Turk & Jew—
> And so, dear Christian Friends, how do you do? [19]

Despite his academic domestication, he retained from his days of Storm and Stress the aura of untamed genius and spread mild terror among his students. One of them, the painter Benjamin Robert Haydon (see Vol. II, p. 83) has left an account of a visit to Fuseli's studio in 1805:

Prince Hoare told me that he had seen Fuseli, who wished me to call on him with my drawings. Fuseli had a great reputation for the terrible. His sublime conception of Uriel and Satan had impressed me when a boy. I had a mysterious awe of him. Prince Hoare's apprehensions lest he might injure my taste or hurt my morals, excited in my mind a notion that he was a sort of gifted wild beast.

My father had the same feeling, and a letter I received from him

[19] G. Keynes, *Poetry and Prose of William Blake,* London, Nonesuch, 1927, p. 855. The epigram is contained in the Rossetti MS among notes related to the *Descriptive Catalogue* of 1809.

just before my calling concluded with these words: ". . . God speed you with the terrible Fuseli."

This sort of preparation made everything worse, and I was quite nervous when the day arrived. I walked away with my drawings up Wardour Street . . . and blundered on, till without knowing how or remembering why I found myself at Fuseli's door! . . . I jerked up the knocker so nervously that it stuck in the air . . . then drove it down with such a devil of a blow that the door rang again. The maid came rushing in astonishment. I followed her into a gallery or show room, enough to frighten anybody at twilight. Galvanized devils—malicious witches brewing their incantations—Satan bridging chaos, and springing upwards like a pyramid of fire—Lady MacBeth—Paolo and Francesca—Falstaff and Mrs. Quickly—humor, pathos, terror, blood, and murder, met one at every look! I expected the floor to give way—I fancied Fuseli himself to be a giant. I heard his footsteps and saw a little bony hand slide round the edge of the door, followed by a little white-headed lion-faced man in an old flannel dressing gown tied round his waist with a piece of rope and upon his head the bottom of Mrs. Fuseli's work basket.

"Well, well," thought I, "I am a match for you at any rate, if bewitching is tried"; but all apprehension vanished on his saying in the mildest and kindest way, "Well, Mr. Haydon, I have heard a great deal of you from Mr. Hoare. Where are your drawings?" In a fright I gave him . . . a sketch of some men pushing a cask into a grocer's shop—Fuseli smiled and said, "By Gode, de fellow does his business at least with energy." [20]

From *Aphorisms on Art*

Although they were published only in 1831, six years after Fuseli's death, the Aphorisms *go back, in their original conception, to 1788. In that year, Fuseli had made an English translation of Lavater's* Regeln zur Selbst- und Menschenkenntnis, *changing the title to* Aphorisms on Man. *This was to be followed by a companion volume, written by Fuseli himself and containing aphorisms on art. A complete manuscript appears to have existed in 1788, but its publication was prevented by a fire. The second and final version was substantially complete by 1818. It included portions of the first version, augmented by new aphorisms which Fuseli had distilled from his academic lectures. Fuseli considered the* Aphorisms *as his most important literary work.*

To the artists and writers of the Storm and Stress, nature manifested itself in character and expression. These two aspects are not exactly

[20] *Autobiography of Benjamin Robert Haydon* (ed. Edmund Blunden), Oxford, n.d., p. 25.

alike: character is the particular form of an individual thing or creature, the product of a unique process of growth; expression, on the other hand, is the direct manifestation of energy, in other words, of a pervasive force which, if raised to its highest intensity, obliterates individual character. Fuseli acknowledged this distinction in his 89th Aphorism:

The being seized by an enormous passion, be it joy or grief, hope or despair, loses the character of its own individual expression and is absorbed by the power of the feature that attracts it: Niobe and her family are assimilated by extreme anguish; Ugolino is pertified by the fate that sweeps his sons. . . .

Both in his art and in his writings on art, Fuseli dwelt on the elemental forces in nature and in human nature, on conflict, terror, and passion. He eliminated from his work all the traces of the specific and spontaneous which mark individual character, and instead developed a highly stylized language. His literary and his graphic work corresponded closely in this respect. In both, extravagant feeling was expressed in gigantic, "petrified," stereotype forms. This gives to Fuseli's Aphorisms *a classicistic flavor which sets them apart from the capricious ramblings of Storm and Stress prose. The* Aphorisms *are verbal monuments, pyramids and obelisks, raised to startle the reader. They have a stylistic affinity with the overwrought monumentality of the art of the French Revolution (see page 126), a fact which points to the underlying connection between the romantic naturalism and the romantic classicism on the last decades of the 18th century.*[21]

3. Art, like love, excludes all competition and absorbs the man.

*   *   *

8. Arrangement presupposes materials: fruits follow the bud and foliage, and judgment the luxuriance of fancy.

*   *   *

13. It is the lot of genius to be opposed, and to be invigorated by opposition: all extremes touch each other; frigid praise and censure wait upon attainable or common powers; but the successful adventurer in the realms of discovery leaps on an unknown or long-lost shore, ennobles it with his name, and grasps immortality.

*   *   *

[21] John Knowles, *The Life and Writings of Henry Fuseli*, London, 1831, **III**, 63 ff.

14. Genius without bias, is a stream without direction: it inundates all, and ends in stagnation.

*   *   *

20. Reality teems with disappointments for him whose sources of enjoyment spring in the elysium of fancy.

*   *   *

22. Determine the principle on which you commence your career of art: some woo the art itself, some its appendages; some confine their view to the present, some extend it to futurity: the butterfly flutters round a meadow; the eagle crosses seas.

*   *   *

24. Circumstances may assist or retard parts, but cannot make them: they are the winds that now blow out a light, now animate a spark to conflagration.

Coroll.—Augustus and Maecenas are said to have made Virgil: what was it, then, that prevented Nerva, Trajan, Adrian, and the two Antonines, from producing at least a Lucan?

*   *   *

28. Genius has no imitator. Some can be poets and painters only at second hand: deaf and blind to the tones and motions of Nature herself, they hear or see her only through some reflected medium of art; they are emboldened by prescription.

*   *   *

30. Mediocrity is formed, and talent submits, to receive prescription; that, the liveried attendant, this, the docile client of a patron's views or whims: but genius, free and unbounded as its *origin,* scorns to receive commands, or in submission, neglects those it received.

Coroll.—The gentle spirit of Raphael embellished the conceits of Bembo and Divizio, to scatter incense round the triple mitre of his prince; and the Vatican became the flattering annals of the court of Julius and Leo: whilst Michael Angelo refused admittance to master and to times, and doomed his purple critic to hell.

*   *   *

35. Art either imitates or copies, selects or transcribes; consults the class, or follows the individual.

*   *   *

36. Imitative art, is either epic or sublime, dramatic or impassioned, historic or circumscribed by truth. The first astonishes, the second moves, the third informs.

*   *   *

42. Beauty alone, fades to insipidity; and like possession cloys.

*   *   *

47. Creation gives, invention finds existence.

*   *   *

59. All conceits, not founded upon probable combinations of nature, are absurd. The *caprici* of Salvator Rosa, and of his imitators, are to the fiends of Michael Angelo, what the paroxysms of a fever are to the sallies of vigorous fancy.

*   *   *

61. Distinguish between boldness and brutality of hand, between the face of beauty and *the bark of a tree.*

*   *   *

62. All mediocrity pretends.

*   *   *

66. Ask not, what is the shape of composition? You may in vain climb the pyramid, wind with the stream, or point the flame; for composition, unbounded like Nature, and her subjects, though resident in all, may be in none of these.

*   *   *

67. The nature of picturesque composition is depth, or to come forward and recede.

Coroll.—Pausias, in painting a sacrifice, foreshortened the victim, and threw its shade on part of the surrounding crowd, to show its height and length.

*   *   *

71. Second thoughts are admissible in painting and poetry only as dressers of the first conception; no great idea was ever formed in fragments.

*   *   *

72. He alone can conceive and compose, who sees the whole at once before him.

*   *   *

103. Fancy not to compose an ideal form by mixing up a mass of promiscuous beauties; for, unless you consulted what was homogeneous and what was possible in Nature, you have hatched only a monster: this, we suppose, was understood by Zeuxis when he collected the beauties of Agrigentum to compose a perfect female.

*   *   *

105. We are more impressed by Gothic than by Greek mythology, because the bands are not yet rent which tie us to its magic: he has a powerful hold of us, who holds us by our superstition or by a theory of honor.

*   *   *

114. He who could have the choice, and should prefer to be the first painter of insects, of flowers, or of drapery, to being the second in the ranks of history, though degraded to the last class of art, would undoubtedly be in the first of men by the decision of Caesar.

*   *   *

118. As far as the medium of an art can be taught, so far is the artist confined to the class of mere mechanics; he only then elevates himself to talent, when he imparts to his method, or to his tool, some unattainable or exclusive excellence of his own.

*   *   *

120. The ear absorbed in harmonies of its own creation, is deaf to all external ones.

*   *   *

122. There is not a bauble thrown by the sportive hand of fashion, which may not be caught with advantage by the hand of art.

Coroll.—Shakespeare has been excused for seeking in the Roman senate what he knew all senates could furnish—a buffoon. Paulo of Verona, with equal strength of argument, may be excused for cramming on the foreground of an assembly or a feast, what he knew a feast or assembly could furnish—a dog, an ape, a scullion, a parrot, or a dwarf.

*   *   *

144. In following too closely a model, there is danger in mistaking the individual for Nature herself; in relying only on the schools, the deviation into manner seems inevitable: what then remains, but to transpose *yourself* into your subject?

*   *   *

148. The superiority of the Greeks seems not so much the result of climate and society, as of the simplicity of their end and the uniformity of their means. If they had schools, the Ionian, that of Athens and of Sicyon appear to have directed their instruction to one grand principle, proportion: this was the stamen which they drew out into one immense connected web; whilst modern art, with its schools of designers, colourists, machinists, eclectics, is but a tissue of adventitious threads. Apollonius and the sculptor of the small Hesperian Hercules in bronze are distinguished only by the degree of execution; whilst M. Angelo and Bernini had no one principle in common but that of making groups and figures.

*   *   *

149. Art among a religious race produces reliques; among a military one, trophies; among a commercial one, articles of trade.

*   *   *

151. The rules of art are either immediately supplied by Nature herself, or selected from the compendiums of her students who are called masters and founders of schools. The imitation of Nature herself leads to style, that of the schools to manner.

Coroll.—The line of Michael Angelo is uniformly grand; character and beauty were admitted only as far as they could be made subservient to grandeur: the child, the female, meanness, deformity were indiscriminately stamped with grandeur; a beggar rose from his hand the patriarch of poverty; the hump of his dwarf is impressed with dignity; his women are moulds of generation; his infants teem with the man, his men are a race of giants. . . .

*　*　*

175. Clearness, freshness, force of colour, are produced by simplicity; one pure, is more than a mixture of many.

*　*　*

176. Colour affects or delights like sound. Scarlet or deep crimson rouses, determines, invigorates the eye, as the war-horn or the trumpet the ear; the flute soothes the ear, as pale celestial blue or rosy red the eye.

*　*　*

177. The colours of sublimity are negative or generic—such is the colouring of Michael Angelo.

*　*　*

194. The forms of virtue are erect, the forms of pleasure undulate: Minerva's drapery descends in long uninterrupted lines; a thousand amorous curves embrace the limbs of Flora.

*　*　*

203. Expect no religion in times when it is easier to meet with a saint than a man; and no art in those that multiply their artists beyond their labourers.

*　*　*

237. Selection is the invention of the landscape painter.

Immanuel Kant (1724–1804)

Kant's approach to art was theoretical in the extreme. He possessed little feeling for the purely visual pleasures, and had no opportunity to see works of painting or sculpture in Königsberg, East Prussia, where he spent his entire life. This practical inexperience occasionally becomes apparent in his odd categorizations, as when, for example, he divides painting into the following classifications: painting proper, landscape gardening, the decoration of rooms with hangings and furniture, and the "art of tasteful dressing with rings, snuff-boxes, etc." His theory of art, nevertheless, was not merely an appendage to his philosophical system. It was, on the contrary, the essential link between his theory of knowledge and his theory of morality, for he believed that aesthetic judgment reconciles the necessity of nature and the freedom of the human mind. His ascetic and disciplined intellectuality set him sharply apart from the enthusiasts of Storm and Stress, but he shared with them the rejection of the superficial rationality and empiricism of the Enlightenment, and the search for the original, creative principle underlying reality. Like the men of Storm and Stress, he had been influenced by Rousseau; unlike them, he did not embrace irrationality, but developed a new theory of reason.

In the Critique of Judgment *(1790), the third and last of his Critiques, Kant formulated a system of aesthetics based on strictly logical analysis and remote from any direct experience of art. Yet several of the concepts which he developed, the ideas of the sublime and of creative genius, for example, resembled those which less systematic minds had been propagating for several decades. Abstract reasoning had led him to insights which corresponded to the intuitive experience of artists and to the taste of the time. The main difference between Kant and his contemporaries of the generation of Storm and Stress lay in the fact that what remained unsystematic psychological speculation, sentiment, or enthusiasm in their work was locked, in his philosophy, into the frame of a coherent theory of knowledge. The revolutionary aspect of this theory, which Kant himself likened to the Copernican hypothesis, lay in its radical subjectivism. While the thought of the Enlightenment had been based on the prevailing conviction that knowledge comes from sense perception, Kant maintained that knowledge is internal: truth resides in the immutable idea, it is not carried to the mind in the flow of sense impressions. The grandiose conceptual abstraction of Kant's philosophy possessed an aesthetic appeal to the men who developed the severe, revolutionary classicism of the last decade of the 18th century.*[22]

From *Critique of Judgment* (1790)

Sublimity is in the Mind of the Judging Subject

. . . Where the size of a natural Object is such that the imagination spends its whole faculty of comprehension upon it in vain, it must

[22] From the translation by J. C. Meredith, *Kant's Critique of Aesthetic Judgment*, Oxford, Clarendon Press, 1911, the following passages have been taken: "Sublimity is in the mind . . . ," p. 104; "Sublimity gives pain . . . ," p. 106; "Nature as Might," p. 108; "Fine art is the art of genius," p. 168. The remaining quotation, "Line more important than color," is from the translation by J. H. Bernard, *Kant's Kritik of Judgment*, New York, 1892, p. 75. For a concise paraphrase of Kant's view of the sublime, see Samuel H. Monk, *The Sublime*, Ann Arbor, University of Michigan, 1960, p. 4.

carry our concept of nature to a supersensible substrate (underlying both nature and our faculty of thought) which is great beyond every standard of sense. Thus, instead of the object, it is rather the cast of the mind in appreciating it that we have to estimate as *sublime*.

This makes it evident that true sublimity must be sought only in the mind of the judging Subject, and not in the Object of nature that occasions this attitude by the estimate formed of it. Who would apply the term "sublime" even to shapeless mountain masses towering one above the other in wild disorder, with their pyramids of ice, or to the dark tempestuous ocean, or such like things? But in the contemplation of them, without any regard to their form, the mind abandons itself to the imagination and to a reason placed, though quite apart from any definite end, in conjunction therewith, and merely broadening its view, and it feels itself elevated in its own estimate of itself on finding all the might of imagination still unequal to its ideas.

Sublimity Gives Pain and Pleasure

The feeling of the sublime is, therefore, at once a feeling of displeasure, arising from the inadequacy of imagination in the aesthetic estimation of magnitude to attain to its estimation by reason, and a simultaneously awakened pleasure, arising from this very judgment of the inadequacy of the greatest faculty of sense being in accord with ideas of reason, so far as the effort to attain to these is for us a law.

The mind feels itself *set in motion* in the representation of the sublime in nature; whereas in the aesthetic judgment upon what is beautiful therein it is in *restful* contemplation. This movement, especially in its inception, may be compared with a vibration, i.e., with a rapidly alternating repulsion and attraction produced by one and the same Object.

Nature as Might

Might is a power which is superior to great hindrances. It is termed *dominion* if it is also superior to the resistance of that which itself possesses might. Nature considered in an aesthetic judgment as might that has no dominion over us, is *dynamically sublime*.

If we are to estimate nature as dynamically sublime, it must be represented as a source of fear.

But we may look upon an object as *fearful,* and yet not be afraid *of* it, if, that is, our estimate takes the form of our simply *picturing to ourselves* the case of our wishing to offer some resistance to it, and recognizing that all such resistance would be quite futile.

One who is in a state of fear can no more play the part of a judge of the sublime of nature than one captivated by inclination and appetite can of the beautiful. He flees from the sight of an object filling him with dread; and it is impossible to take delight in terror that is seriously entertained. Hence the agreeableness arising from the cessation of an uneasiness is *a state of joy*. But this, depending upon deliverance from a danger, is a rejoicing accompanied with a resolve never again to put oneself in the way of the danger: in fact we do not like bringing back to mind how we felt on that occasion—not to speak of going in search of an opportunity for experiencing it again.

Bold, overhanging, and, as it were, threatening rocks, thunderclouds piled up the vault of heaven, borne along with flashes and peals, volcanoes in all their violence of destruction, hurricanes leaving desolation in their track, the boundless ocean rising with rebellious force, the high waterfall of some mighty river, and the like, make our power of resistance of trifling moment in comparison with their might. But, provided our own position is secure, their aspect is all the more attractive for its fearfulness; and we readily call these objects sublime, because they raise the forces of the soul above the height of vulgar commonplace, and discover within us a power of resistance of quite another kind, which gives us courage to be able to measure ourselves against the seeming omnipotence of nature.

Fine Art is the Art of Genius

Genius is the talent . . . which gives the rule to art. Since talent, as an innate productive faculty of the artist, belongs itself to nature, we may put it this way: *Genius* is the innate mental aptitude . . . *through which* nature gives the rule to art.

Every one is agreed on the point of the complete opposition between genius and the *spirit of imitation*. Now since learning is nothing but imitation, the greatest ability, or aptness as a pupil, is still, as such, not equivalent to genius. Even though a man weaves his own thoughts or fancies, instead of merely taking in what others have thought, and even though he go so far as to bring fresh gains to art and science, this does not afford a valid reason for calling such a man of *brains,* and often great brains, a *genius.*

Despite the marked difference that distinguishes mechanical art, as an art merely depending upon industry and learning, from fine art, as that of genius, there is still no fine art in which something mechanical, capable of being at once comprehended and followed in obedience to rules, and consequently something *academic* does not constitute the essential condition of the art. For the thought of something as end must be present, or else its product would not be ascribed to an art at all, but would be a mere product of chance. But the effectuation of an end necessitates determinate rules which we cannot venture to dispense with. Now, seeing that originality of talent is one (though not the sole) essential factor that goes to make up the character of genius, shallow minds fancy that the best evidence they can give of their being full-blown geniuses is by emancipating themselves from all academic constraint of rules, in the belief that one cuts a finer figure on the back of an ill-tempered than of a trained horse. Genius can do no more than furnish rich *material* for products of fine art; its elaboration and its *form* require a talent academically trained, so that it may be employed in such a way as to stand the test of judgment. But, for a person to hold forth and pass sentence like a genius in matters that fall to the province of the most patient rational investigation, is ridiculous in the extreme.

Line is More Important than Color

In painting, sculpture, and in all the formative arts—in architecture, and horticulture, so far as they are beautiful arts—the *delineation* is the essential thing; and here it is not what gratifies in sensation but what pleases by means of its form that is fundamental for taste. The colors which light up the sketch belong to the charm; they may indeed enliven the object for sensation, but they cannot make it worthy of contemplation and beautiful. In most cases they are rather limited by the requirements of the beautiful form; and even where charm is permissible it is ennobled solely by this.

Every form of the objects of sense (both of external sense and also mediately of internal) is either *figure* or *play*. In the latter case it is either play of figures (in space, viz., pantomime and dancing), or the mere play of sensations (in time). The *charm* of colors or of the pleasant tones of an instrument may be added; but the *delineation* in the first case and the composition in the second constitute the proper object of the pure judgment of taste. To say that the purity of colors and of tones, or their variety and contrast, seems to add to beauty, does not mean that they supply a homogeneous addition to our satisfaction in the form because they are pleasant in themselves; but they do so, because they make the form more exactly, definitely, and completely, intuitible, and besides by their charm excite the representation, while they awaken and fix our attention on the object itself.

THE PATHOLOGY OF GENIUS

The generation which came to maturity in the 1770's reacted against the scepticism of the Enlightenment with a fresh curiosity concerning the occult and esoteric. Jakob Boehme's arcane writings and Emanuel Swedenborg's prophecies were widely read; theosophy and mysticism attracted converts; honest men devoted themselves to spiritism and alchemy, while swindlers and miracle-workers went from town to town to exploit the gullible public. Lavater (see page 86), Mesmer, and Cagliostro held the stage in turn. Rosicrucians, illuminati, and Free Masons competed with one another. Experimental science and crass charlatanry flourished side by side. The current of counter-Enlightenment amounted to a revulsion from the more banal forms of rationalism. It also expressed a desire to penetrate beneath the surface of common matter and common sense to the sources of reality. In the arts, the new attitude manifested itself in a growing impatience with academic routine and in the cult of creative genius. Some considered genius as a natural force working through the artist, others thought it to be of supernatural origin, a demonic or divine possession, a form of madness. In some exceptional artists, the visionary powers of genius were observed to assume the involuntary, quasi-objective character of hallucination or ghostly visitation. Such artists saw spirits, and it is difficult to decide today whether these visions resulted from a predisposition not uncommon at the time, and hence to be considered as "normal," or whether they were symptoms of individual derangement.

Franz Xaver Messerschmidt's (1736–1783) "Egyptian Heads"

Messerschmidt began his career brilliantly, as a sculptor serving the Imperial court and the high nobility of Vienna, and as a teacher at the Academy. He had a particular gift for portraiture and was a consummate technician. About 1770, he appears to have suffered an illness which, in the opinion of his colleagues and superiors, unfitted him for teaching, though it did not interfere with his art. He felt persecuted and mistreated, resigned his appointments, left Vienna, and settled in Pressburg. Here, living the life of a hermit, he devoted himself obsessively to the sculpting of a series of sixty-four heads representing his own features contorted into strange grimaces. The extreme eccentricity of these works, and the rumor that Messerschmidt communicated with ghosts, attracted visitors to his lonely studio. One of these, the publicist C. F. Nicolai, left an account of such a visit, in 1781, which is all the more curious in that it presents "mad" genius as seen through the eyes of an especially prosaic exponent of the Enlightenment.[23]

Messerschmidt was a man of fiery imagination and powerful, sanguine constitution, who, since early youth, had nearly always lived in solitude and perfect chastity. He told me this himself, to prove that he really did see spirits . . . rather than merely imagined them. To me, it seemed to prove just the contrary. . . . I tried to sound out Messerschmidt, to discover how these notions were related in his mind. He spoke reticently, and not very clearly, and it appeared that he had a rather confused notion of his own thoughts. But I managed to get out of him that he was absolutely convinced that spirits did in fact frighten and molest him, especially at night. . . . And he added that he had long been unable to understand why he, who had always lived a chaste life, should have to endure so much torment. . . . But, after much thought on the subject, he had finally perfected a system by means of which anyone could gain control over the spirits. The good man started from the perfectly sound premise that all things in this world stand in a particular relationship to one another and that all effects result from sufficient causes. He expressed this, somewhat vaguely and ambiguously, as follows: all the world is ruled by proportion; if one were able to produce in oneself proportions equivalent or superior to those of another being, then he ought to be able to produce effects equivalent or superior to the effects of the other. From this half-understood principle, compounded with his foolish notion about spirits and his knowledge of art, he made up a seemingly profound system, part nonsense, part method, which, in the manner of people whose reason has been overwhelmed by their imagination, he considered infallible. . . . He believed, furthermore, that the proportions of the head correspond in every detail to the proportions of the various parts of the body. . . . When he felt pains in his abdomen or thigh, he imagined that this resulted from the fact that he was at that moment working on some particular part of the face of a marble or lead bust which corresponded to these particular portions of the lower part of the body. . . . Since his fantasy was filled with spirits, he conceived the idea of a special Spirit of Proportion. Believing, in his vanity, that he had made unheard-of discoveries concerning proportions and their effects, and feeling abdominal pains . . . while on the point of making his

---

[23] C. Friedrich Nicolai, *Reisebeschreibung durch Deutschland und die Schweiz im Jahre 1781*, VI, 401, quoted by Ernst Kris, "Die Charakterköpfe des Franz Xaver Messerschmidt," *Jahrbuch der kunsthistorischen Sammlungen*, Vienna, NF VI, 1932, 224 ff.

discoveries, he fancied that it was the Spirit of Proportion who, envious of his perfect knowledge, was causing him this pain. Being a determined person, he gathered up his courage to overcome the imaginary evil spirit. He made every effort to penetrate more deeply into the mystery of relationships, in order that he might defeat the spirit, rather than be defeated by him. He went so far with his absurd theory as to imagine that he would attain perfection in this matter if he pinched himself in various parts of the body, particularly under his lower right rib, accompanying this with a grimace correctly proportioned to the pinch. He was confirmed in this madness by an English visitor whom he regarded as the only other person to have understood the system. He told me that this Englishman, unable to express himself in German, had indicated the precise spot on his exposed thigh which corresponded to the part of a head which Messerschmidt was about to execute. This, he said, had given him absolute certainty that his system was unquestionably correct.

He thereupon set to work, pinched himself and grimaced in front of the mirror, and thought that he experienced the marvellous effects of his control over the spirits. Delighted with his system, he resolved to pass it on to posterity by means of portraits of the grimacing proportions. It was his opinion that there were sixty-four basic varieties of grimaces. When I visited him, he had completed sixty different heads, some in marble, others in a mixture of lead and pewter, most of them the size of life. He had spent no fewer than eleven years in this unfortunate labor, working with astonishing patience. All the heads were self-portraits. I saw him at work on the sixty-first head. He would look into the mirror every half minute and assume precisely the grimace he wanted. Considered as works of art, the heads are admirable masterpieces, especially the more natural ones. But the majority represent strangely contorted faces, with lips tightly compressed. I should have been at a loss to explain the reason for these odd distortions, if Messerschmidt had not initiated me into the rules underlying his crazy method. He told me that human beings ought to conceal the red of their lips entirely, because animals never show theirs. A curious reason! I countered by saying that men are not animals. But he had a ready answer: animals, he said, are superior to men in that they see and recognize many aspects of nature which remain hidden to men. . . .

William Blake's (1757–1827) Visionary Portraits

William Blake, from earliest childhood, possessed the gift of spiritual vision. At the age of four, he saw the face of God pressed against the pane of his window, and after the death of his brother, Robert, he often conversed with his spirit and was instructed by him in a new method of relief etching. Blake's visions, like those of Messerschmidt, were directly relevant to his art. His imagination presented to him the faces and figures of his ghostly visitors in the sharply contoured, strangely stylized forms in which he drew them. What other artists achieved through a conscious effort of arrangement and design, Blake received ready-made. The clarity of his visions confirmed him in his dislike of the "blotting and blurring" Venetians, of Rembrandt and Reynolds.

Blake generally drew his visionary heads at night, often in the company of his friends, John Linnell and John Varley, the astrologer. It was they who supplied Blake's biographer, Allan Cunningham, with the information on which the following account is based.[24]

To describe the conversations which Blake held in prose with demons and in verse with angels, would fill volumes, and an ordinary gallery could not contain all the heads which he drew of his visionary visitants. That all this was real, he himself most sincerely believed; nay, so infectious was his enthusiasm, that some acute and sensible persons who heard him expatiate, shook their heads, and hinted that he was an extraordinary man, and that there might be something in the matter. One of his brethren, an artist of some note, employed him frequently in drawing the portraits of those who appeared to him in visions. The most propitious time for those "angel-visits" was from nine at night till five in the morning; and so docile were his spiritual sitters, that they appeared at the wish of his friends. Sometimes, however, the shape which he desired to draw was long in appearing, and he sat with his pencil and paper ready and his eyes idly roaming in vacancy; all at once the vision came upon him, and he began to work like one possessed.

He was requested to draw the likeness of William Wallace—the eye of Blake sparkled, for he admired heroes. "William Wallace!" he exclaimed, "I see him now, there, there, how noble he looks—reach me my things!" Having drawn for some time, with the same care of hand and steadiness of eye, as if a living sitter had been before him, Blake stopped suddenly and said, "I cannot finish him—Edward the First has stept in between him and me." "That's lucky," said his friend, "for I want the portrait of Edward too." Blake took another sheet of paper, and sketched the features of Plantagenet; upon which his Majesty politely vanished, and the artist finished the head of Wallace.

The friend who obliged me with these anecdotes, on observing the interest which I took in the subject, said, "I know much about Blake—I was his companion for nine years. I have sat beside him from ten at night till three in the morning, sometimes slumbering and sometimes waking,

[24] Cf. Mona Wilson, *The Life of William Blake*, London, Nonesuch, 1927, pp. 256 ff.

but Blake never slept; he sat with a pencil and paper drawing portraits of those whom I most desired to see. I will show you, sir, some of these works." He took out a large book filled with drawings, opened it, and continued, "Observe the poetic fervour of that face—it is Pindar as he stood a conqueror in the Olympic games. And this lovely creature is Corinna, who conquered in poetry in the same place. That Lady is Lais, the courtesan—with the impudence which is part of her profession, she stept in between Blake and Corinna, and he was obliged to paint her to get her away." . . .

He closed the book, and taking out a small panel from a private drawer, said, "This is the last which I shall show you; but it is the greatest curiosity of all. Only look at the splendour of the colouring and the original character of the thing!" "I see," said I, "a naked figure with a strong body and a short neck—with burning eyes which long for moisture, and a face worthy of a murderer, holding a bloody cup in its clawed hands, out of which it seems eager to drink. I never saw any shape so strange, nor did I ever see any colouring so curiously splendid—a kind of glistening green and dusky gold, beautifully varnished. But what in the world is it?" "It is a ghost, sir—the ghost of a flea—a spiritualization of the thing!" "He saw this in a vision then," I said. "I'll tell you all about it, sir. I called on him one evening, and found Blake more than usually excited. He told me he had seen a wonderful thing—the ghost of a flea! 'And did you make a drawing of him?' I inquired. 'No, indeed,' said he, 'I wish I had, but I shall, if he appears again!' He looked earnestly into a corner of the room, and then said, 'Here he is—reach me my things—I shall keep my eye on him. There he comes! his eager tongue whisking out of his mouth, a cup in his hand to hold blood and covered with a scaly skin of gold and green';—as he described him so he drew him.''

FREEDOM FROM PATRONAGE

Genius does not tolerate patronage. Until the middle of the 18th century, artists had generally courted the wealthy and powerful, and accepted with resignation the occasional humiliations which attended their servile role. But as the century wore on, they showed themselves less willing to sacrifice dignity and independence for material rewards. Instead of appealing to individual benefactors, they now preferred to address themselves to the general public.

William Hogarth's (1697–1764) "The No Dedication," which parodies the language and lists the objects of conventional dedicatory flattery, gives expression to the new attitude. It was found among his papers after his death, and is supposed to have been written by way of preface for his autobiography or for some projected treatise on art.[25]

The No Dedication

Not dedicated to any Prince in Christendom for fear it might be thought a
   Bold piece of arrogance.
Not dedicated to any man of quality for fear it might be thought too
   affecting.
Not dedicated to any learned body
of men of either of the universities, or the
Royal Society, for fear it might be thought
An uncommon piece of vanity.
Nor dedicated to any particular friend
for fear of offending another.
Therefore dedicated to nobody
But if for once we may suppose
Nobody to be everybody as everybody
Is often found to be nobody, then is this work
Dedicated to anybody
                    By their most humble
                    and devoted, W. Hogarth.

Giovanni Battista Piranesi (1720–1778)

While in Rome, in 1751, James Caulfield, 1st Earl of Charlemont, an ambitious politician, traveller, and patron of the arts, was invited by the great draftsman and antiquarian Piranesi (see page 26) to support the publication of a volume of plates illustrating Roman monuments. Lord Charlemont agreed to accept, and pay for, a dedicatory frontispiece, a common form of sponsorship. In the course of executing the work, Piranesi expanded its size to four volumes. Lord Charlemont, who was consulted, appeared to agree to receive four dedications, instead of one, and to increase his stipend proportionately. But when the work was published, in 1756, under the title of Le Antichita Romane, *Lord Charlemont's agent in Rome offered Piranesi an insultingly small sum. Injured in his pride even more than in his financial interest, Piranesi sent three letters to his patron, all of which remained unanswered. He then erased the dedication to Charlemont and, to justify his conduct, took the unprecedented step of having his letters printed, to exhibit to the public*

25 Cf. Marjorie Bowen, *William Hogarth*, New York, Appleton-Century, 1936, p. 319.

at large the spectacle of a noble patron's meanness and of an artist's dignity. The following passages are taken from the first of the letters, dated August 25, 1756.[26]

From *Letters to Lord Charlemont* (1756)

. . . I believe that I have completed a work which will pass on to posterity and which will endure so long as there are men curious to know the ruins which remain of the most famous city in the universe. . . . This work is not of the kind which remains buried in the crowded shelves of libraries. Its four folio volumes comprise a new system of the monuments of ancient Rome. It will be deposited in many public libraries throughout Europe, and in particular in that of the Most Christian King. And there is reason to suppose that the name of its author will pass on to posterity together with his work. . . . Is it not a very unpleasant circumstance, then, that having invested my thoughts, talents, work, and purse, that having labored unceasingly for eight years to make this work worthy of Your Lordship, I should now be insulted by a man [Charlemont's agent] who, to do me greater injury, arms himself with the credit which he has with Your Lordship? . . . The time has come, therefore, to think of saving my honor. Should I be forced to suppress the Dedication, I beg Your Lordship not to take this as an offense against your forebears, but as a reparation which is owed to me. For when the story of my life is written, along with that of other artists, I do not want to stand accused of having been a flatterer . . . who was held in low esteem even by those on whom he lavished his praise. If Your Lordship do not loosen my tongue, if you do not render me justice and protect me against calumny . . . then I cannot, as a man of honor, or without making myself ridiculous, call you a protector of the arts and myself an artist who received your protection. And if I have seemed to call you so, in the seventy copies of my work which have already been sold, then I must face the painful necessity of having to accuse my own foolishness and of trying to vindicate myself before the world. For I must ask you to bear in mind that, as a nobleman must consider his ancestors, an artist who will leave his name to posterity must consider his own reputation and that of his descendants. A nobleman is the latest of his name, an artist the first of his; both must act with equal delicacy. If I should ever have to publish this letter, which I should do only with the greatest regret, I implore those who read it, posterity as well as you, My Lord, to believe that I do not lack the deep respect which I owe Your

---

[26] The text is contained in a few copies of *Le Antichita Romane* and in a separate pamphlet which Piranesi published under the title of *Lettere di Giustificazione scritti a Milord Charlemont*, Rome, 1757. The first of Piranesi's three letters, dated August 25, 1756, is the one here quoted in part.

Lordship. I do not claim equality for your name and mine, only for our reputations, for this is something which must be equally precious to all men, of whatever profession they might be. . . .

Reynolds and Blake on Patronage

In delivering the first of his Discourses *(1769), Sir Joshua Reynolds still conformed to the convention of servile praise for royal and aristocratic patronage, describing it as a main circumstance "from which honour and prosperity can probably arise" for the artists of the newly founded Academy:* [27]

. . . There is a general desire among our Nobility to be distinguished as lovers and judges of the Arts; there is a greater superfluity of wealth among the people to reward the professors; and, above all, we are patronized by a Monarch, who, knowing the value of science and of elegance, thinks every Art worthy of his notice, that tends to soften and humanize the mind.

After so much has been done by His Majesty, it will be wholly our fault, if our progress is not in some degree correspondent to the wisdom and generosity of the Institution: let us shew our gratitude in our diligence, that, though our merit may not answer his expectations, yet, at least, our industry may deserve his protection.

A generation later (1808), William Blake, in annotating Reynolds' Discourses *(see page 34), savagely indicted the system of patronage for its economical insufficiency, its social condescension, and its intellectual arrogance.*[28]

Who will Dare to Say that Polite Art is Encouraged or Either Wished or Tolerated in a Nation where The Society for the Encouragement of Art Suffer'd Barry to Give them his Labour for Nothing, A Society Composed of the Flower of the English Nobility & Gentry?— Suffering an Artist to Starve while he Supported Really what They, under Pretence of Encouraging, were Endeavouring to Depress.—Barry told me that while he Did that Work, he Lived on Bread & Apples.

O Society for Encouragement of Art! O King & Nobility of Eng-

27 Robert R. Wark (ed.), *Sir Joshua Reynolds, Discourses on Art,* Huntington Library, San Marino, 1959, p. 3.

28 G. Keynes (ed.), *Poetry and Prose of William Blake,* London, Nonesuch, 1927, p. 971. A fuller selection from Blake's annotations is given below, page 120.

land! Where have you hid Fuseli's Milton? Is Satan troubled at his Exposure? . . .

Liberality! we want not Liberality. We want a Fair Price & Proportionate Value & a General Demand for Art.

Let not that Nation where Less than Nobility is the Reward, Pretend that Art is Encouraged by that Nation. Art is First in Intellectuals & Ought to be First in Nations.

Continuing his denunciation of patronage in the manuscript of the Public Address *(1810), Blake proclaimed the sovereignty of artists in the language of revolutionary oratory:* [29]

Rubens's Luxembourg Gallery is Confessed on all hands to be the work of a Blockhead: it bears this Evidence on its face. . . . If all the Princes in Europe, like Louis XIV & Charles the first, were to Patronize such Blockheads, I, William Blake, a Mental Prince, should decollate and Hang their Souls as Guilty of Mental High Treason. . . . The wretched State of the Arts in this Country & in Europe, originating in the wretched State of Political Science, which is the Science of Sciences, Demands a firm & determinate conduct on the part of Artists to resist the Contemptable Counter Arts Establish'd by such contemptible Politicians as Louis XIV & originally set on foot by Venetian Picture traders. . . . Imagination is My World; this world of Dross is beneath my Notice & beneath the Notice of the Public. I demand therefore of the Amateurs of art the Encouragement which is my due; if they continue to refuse, theirs is the loss, not mine, & theirs is the Contempt of Posterity. I have Enough in the Approbation of my Fellow laborers; this is my glory & exceeding great reward. I go on & nothing can hinder my course:

> and in Melodious Accents I
> Will sit me down & Cry I, I.

Asmus Jakob Carstens (1754–1798) and the Prussian Minister

The painter Asmus Carstens, a Danish subject, held a teaching position at the Prussian Academy in Berlin. In 1792, he received a fairly generous travel stipend and other grants which were to enable him to spend three years in Rome at the Prussian state's expense. In return, Carstens undertook to report to the Ministry concerning his progress, and to send some of his work to Berlin for exhibition. He was irritatingly slow in fulfilling both these obligations. After an initial extension of

[29] *Ibid.,* p. 818.

*his leave, he at last informed the Ministry that he wished to break his
contract with the Academy, in order to remain in Rome indefinitely. The
Minister, Baron von Heinitz, thereupon sent him a letter of reproach
and dismissal, pointing out to Carstens that "the unilateral cancellation
of mutual obligations is not customary anywhere, least of all in Prussia."
In his* Reply to Baron von Heinitz *(February 20, 1796) Carstens protested
against the threatened reprisals and asserted the right, or even duty, of
artists to further their personal development, regardless of social obligations. The letter documents the emancipation of artists toward the end
of the 18th century, not only from official patronage, but also from some
of the social and legal restraints which bind other men.*[30]

Since you speak of mutual obligations, I must state that I have
never been under any obligation to the Academy. Independent of its
administration, I gave good instruction in return for a mediocre salary.
I am not even a member. If I am obligated to anyone, it is to your Excellency. But this mutual obligation is now dissolved, as, in justice to myself, I have already been obliged to point out. . . .

Besides, I must tell you Excellency that I belong to Humanity, not
to the Academy of Berlin. It was never my intention, nor did I ever
promise to become the life-long serf of an Academy, in return for a few
years' pension granted me for the development of my talent. It is only
here [in Rome] that I can properly train myself, surrounded by the best
works of art in the world, and I shall continue with all my strength to
justify myself in the eyes of the world through my own works. I renounce
all benefits, preferring poverty, an uncertain future, and perhaps an
infirm and helpless old age, my body beginning already to show signs
of debility, in order to do my duty to art and fulfill my calling as an
artist. My capabilities were entrusted to me by God; I must husband
them conscientiously, so that when He asks me to give an accounting of
myself, I shall not have to answer: Lord, the talent which you entrusted
to me I have buried in Berlin.

Since I have always known and valued your Excellency as a lover
of the truth, I have not hesitated to write the truth freely, and I am
ready, if necessary, to assert it in public, to justify myself to the world, as
I feel justified in my own conscience.

With deepest respect, I remain
Your Excellency's devoted
Carstens.

[30] Carl Ludwig Fernow, *Das Leben des Künstlers Asmus Jakob Carstens,* Leipzig,
1806, pp. 190 ff. (von Heinitz' letter) and pp. 199 ff. (Carstens' letter).

The Public at Large as Patron of the Arts

The insufficiency of patronage was most painfully felt by history painters whose large compositions were the most costly and laborious to produce, and the most difficult to sell. To make up for the lack or uncertainty of official support, artists occasionally tried to address themselves directly to the public. In England, where official patronage was very limited, it was a common practice for artists to sell reproductive prints of their paintings, or to exhibit individual pictures to the public for a fee. The English engraver Valentine Green (1739–1813) *in his* Review of the Polite Arts in France . . . Compared with their Present State in England . . . in a Letter to Sir Joshua Reynolds *(1782) expressed a common complaint about both these practices which many artists found humiliating:* [31]

. . . Neither is it to be expected, that the series of Subjects from the English History, carrying on by Mr. West, of which the *Death of General Wolfe* began, and *the Battles of the Boyne,* and *La Hogue,* are a continuation; nor yet *the Death of the late Earl of Chatham,* by Mr. Copley, should be ascribed to Public Patronage given to Historical Painting. In neither of these instances has it been applied. The first Subjects were presented by the Painters. . . . The second was sent out of the kingdom to a foreigner. The others were Works of Speculation, begun by the Artists themselves, without commission, or the least dependance of their ever being disposed of. If, in any of these cases, the Artists had not been known to possess abilities worthy to have been employed, the question would have been unnecessary for me to put at this time—how it comes to pass, that, in the most peremptory and decided language, it is insisted on, that the most liberal encouragement is given to the English Artists? Is it because a *Guinea* is subscribed to the purchase of a *Print* from those Pictures, for which the Painters, in superaddition to their own speculative labours, venture on the heavy expences attending the laborious operations of Engraving them? Or is it, because from motives of prudence, impelled by the neglect they have experienced, they are unwillingly forced on the expedient of challenging attention, by offering those Works to public view, and setting the price of a *Shilling* on the humiliating Practice? But this Patronage is unique, it belongs only to ourselves; and, in addition to its other merits, is likely

[31] Valentine Green, *A Review of the Polite Arts in France . . . Compared with their Present State in England . . . in a letter to Sir Joshua Reynolds,* London, 1782, p. 49.

to produce this farther brilliant effect, namely, the making Marchands d'Estampes of our first men of Genius, and reducing the study of their Professions to *Connoisseurship in proof impressions from Engravings.*

David on Public Exhibitions

It is curious to note that, nearly twenty years later, the French painter Jacques Louis David (see pp. 114, 130) used the very examples which Green had cited in his denunciation of individual exhibitions in order to justify his own public exhibition of "The Battle of Romans and Sabines" *(1800). David had completed this painting in 1799. Still in partial disgrace, as a former leading Jacobin, and perhaps afraid of chicanery from the officials in charge of the regular Salon, David decided to offer his work to public view, for an admission charge, in a special, privately arranged exhibition at the Louvre. The picture remained on view from 1800 until 1804, earning him the very considerable sum of 65,000 francs. Since individual exhibitions for the artist's personal benefit were contrary to French usage, David felt it necessary to justify himself to his visitors in a pamphlet from which the following passages are taken. It might be noted that while such exhibitions remained fairly uncommon outside France—Carstens had privately exhibited his works to Roman connoisseurs in 1795, and Blake held an exhibition in London in 1809 (see page 150)—a few French artists imitated David, among them Géricault (who exhibited his* Medusa *in England), Horace Vernet, and, ultimately, Courbet.[32]*

Antiquity has ever been the school of modern painters and the source from which they have drawn the beauties of their art. We try to imitate the ancients in the genius of their conceptions, the purity of their design, the expression of their faces and the grace of their forms. Could we not go one step further and also imitate their customs and institutions, in order to raise the arts to a state of perfection?

There is nothing new about exhibitions in which the work of a particular painter is shown to his fellow-citizens for a fee. The learned Abbé Barthelemy mentions in his *Voyage of the Young Anacharsis* that the famous Zeuxis collected a fee from those who viewed his works, and in this way grew so rich that he was able to give many of his masterpieces to his country, saying that no private individual could afford them. . . . The custom of public exhibition thus prevailed among the Greeks; we need not fear that we shall go wrong if we follow them.

[32] The passage is taken from the introduction of the pamphlet which bears the title *Le Tableau des Sabines, exposé publiquement au Palais National . . . par le Citoyen David,* Paris, Didot, 1800, p. 1 ff.

In our time, this practice is observed in England. . . . The pictures of the Death of General Wolfe and the Death of Chatham by Benjamin West, our contemporary, have earned him immense sums in that country. One-man exhibitions have been held in England for a long time; it was Van Dyck who introduced them in the last century. The public came in crowds to admire his works, and he managed to amass a large fortune in this way.

Is there not a great deal of justice and wisdom in this arrangement which allows artists to support themselves by drawing on their resources, and to enjoy the noble independence which belongs to genius . . . ? What better way is there of deriving an honorable benefit from the fruits of one's work than to submit it to the judgment of the public, and to expect in return only those rewards which public approval will bestow? If the work is mediocre, the public will soon have judged it so. The artist, having gained neither glory nor fortune, will be taught by this severe lesson to correct his faults and to seek better ways of arresting the public's attention.

Of all the arts which genius practices, painting is surely the one which calls for the greatest sacrifice. It is not unusual for the completion of a history painting to require as many as three or four years of work. I shall not dwell on the preliminary expenditures which painters must incur; the cost of costumes and models alone is very considerable. There can be no doubt that these difficulties have discouraged many artists. It is possible that some of the masterpieces which their genius conceived have been lost to us, because poverty prevented them from being executed. I shall go even further and ask: how many honorable and virtuous painters who would never have lent their brush to any but elevating moral subjects have been forced by want to degrade and lower themselves? They have prostituted their talent for the money of Phryne and Lais. It was their indigence which caused them to become guilty; their talent, destined to elevate morals, contributed to their corruption.

I should be happy if my example were to initiate the custom of public exhibition, thus helping to protect men of talent from poverty and contributing to the return of the arts to their true purpose, which is to serve morality and to elevate the soul. . . . The means for moving the human heart are a great secret, they could give a powerful impetus to the nation's energy and character. Who can deny that the French people have until now remained strangers to art and have lived among the arts without partaking of them? Whenever painting or sculpture achieved a rare masterpiece, it fell immediately into the hands of a rich man, often at a low price; it was jealously guarded by him, as his exclusive property, to be shared only with a few friends and to be denied to the rest of society. The system of exhibitions would at least allow the public to share the riches of genius, in return for a small fee. The public could then learn about the arts, to which it is not so indifferent as some believe. This would enlighten it and improve its taste. For though the public lacks the experience necessary for deciding about the finer and more difficult points of art, its judgment, which is always inspired by nature and prompted by feeling, can give pleasure and even insight to artists who know how to use it.

How painful and sad it is, for men sincerely devoted to art and to their country, to see many precious works go to foreign nations, when the nation which produced them has scarcely had the chance of becoming acquainted with them. Public exhibitions will tend to preserve master-works for the fortunate country which produced them. . . .

The objection will probably be raised that every nation has its own customs, and that the custom of holding public exhibitions of art has never become accepted in France. To this I can only reply that I am unable to explain the contradictions of human conduct. But I should like to know what dramatic author would not give the greatest possible publicity to his work, or would hesitate to receive part of the admission charge paid by the spectators, in exchange for the emotions and pleasures which he gave to them by his depiction of man's passions and foibles? And I should like to know, too, whether a musical composer, having imparted soul and life to a lyrical poem, would blush to share with the author of the poem the profits derived from its representation? What is honorable to one profession ought not to be humiliating to another. . . .

AGAINST THE ACADEMY

The English engraver Valentine Green wrote in 1782, after a visit to France, ". . . At the present moment, the foundation of their School of Art cannot be shaken, but with the extremest convulsion of the State: nor will any of its Sovereigns be hardy enough to encounter the odium that would be attendant on any hostile proceedings against an institution whence so much honor has been derived to the nation. At this moment its vigour is unimpaired, and its principles are as active as in the time of the fourteenth Louis, so far as regards its funds, and its cultivation of genius." [33] *The Enlightenment had put the necessity of academic institutions beyond serious question. Criticism of the Academy, nevertheless,*

[33] Valentine Green, *op. cit.*, p. 10.

became more and more frequent in the latter half of the 18th century. It came from two quite different quarters. On the one hand, there were those who disliked the Academy's monopolistic control of the means of education and patronage, who deplored the tyrannical nature of its power, and called for a reorganization of its internal constitution. Some detractors, on the other hand, found fault with the educational methods used by the Academy; a few radical critics went so far as to deny that art could be taught by method and rule and regarded the institution as essentially harmful. Critics of the first kind had a political or economic bias. Their aim was reform and renewal, even if this were to necessitate a temporary suspension of the Academy, such as occurred during the French Revolution. Critics of the second kind were motivated by more fundamental, philosophical, or artistic considerations. Their goal was the Academy's permanent abolition.

Antoine Quatremère de Quincy (1775–1849) on the Academy

An academically trained sculptor, winner of the Academy's Rome Prize, Quatremère de Quincy became an archaeologist and publicist. After the outbreak of the Revolution, he was elected to the Legislative Assembly in which he frequently represented the interest of the artists and the cause of academic reform. His Considérations sur les arts du dessin *(1791), from which the following excerpts are taken, contains a detailed criticism of the academy and an elaborate plan for its improvement.[34] It represents an attitude which is distinctly more moderate than that of Louis David (see page 115).*

There still exists—I almost said: there existed—a sovereignty of artists known under the name of Royal Academy of Painting and Sculpture. Its internal organization seems democratic, but is so only after the fashion of the aristocracy of Venice. This body has the right of giving public instruction in the arts; this is the least of its prerogatives. It also is the final judge of all talents and holds the power of life and death over all reputations. It possesses the ability to increase or reduce the number of its appointments, to open or close its doors at will, to let its enemies languish in obscurity, and to raise its favorites from insignificance. Supreme arbiter of public opinion, simply by virtue of its power to admit or to reject, it stamps with the mark of honor the servile brow which inclines under its yoke, or brands with disgrace the independent who dares to oppose it. Sole dispenser of all fame, exclusive proprietor of all honorific privileges, of all means for gaining a reputa-

[34] Antoine C. Quatremère de Quincy, *Seconde Suite aux Considérations sur les arts du dessin*, Paris, 1791; the passages quoted occur on pages 3 and 12.

tion, of all public encouragements, it forces all men of talent to vie for its favor, it tyrannizes taste, it controls all dispositions and imperiously attracts to itself all those who have an inclination for the arts. Since it combines, in vicious union, the characters of school and academy, the right to shape and to reward talent, this body exercises, unopposed, all material and moral power. A truly vicious circle of influence, it attracts public attention to those whom it chooses as its members, and by manipulating public opinion determines the stature of artists. Perpetual seminary of incurable prejudices, it prohibits every debate and suppresses all spirit of innovation. . . .

In my opinion, the main defects of the present Academy are the following three:

1. The despotic authority of a material and moral kind which, by virtue of its power, it holds over the arts and the artists.

2. The pettiness and levelling influence of its teaching on the spirit of students and on the development of their talents.

3. The revolting inequality which results from the privileges, both practical and ideal, which the Academy possesses, and which cause in those who benefit from them, as well as those who are deprived of them, passions that are inimical to the progress of art.

Jacques Louis David (1748–1825) and the Suppression of the Academy (1793)

The events which led to the closing of the French Academy of Painting and Sculpture in August of 1793, at the height of the Jacobin regime, originated in a quarrel among the members over matters of rights and privileges, rather than over principles of art. As early as 1789, the two lower ranks of the membership, the agrées *and the* académiciens, *had begun to contest the authority and special privileges of the* officers, *the ruling body of the Academy. The painter Louis David (see pp. 111, 130), himself an* académicien, *or member of the middle rank, acted from the start as the elected spokesman of the dissidents. Their aim was at first merely to liberalize, rather than close, the Academy, but the momentum of revolution rapidly magnified the dispute, and drew the opposing factions into the mainstream of political events: what had started as an attempt at organizational reform became an attack on the "citadel of privilege." David was propelled into the center of the political storm.*

With intelligent ruthlessness, the rebellious Academicians went over the heads of their officers and of the Ministry, to address their demands first to the Commune of Paris (February 1790), then to the National Assembly (June 1790), and finally to the Jacobin Club (July 1790). The

*plan of supplanting the "aristocratic" Academy with a revolutionary
Commune of the Arts gradually took shape. In September of 1792, David
entered the National Convention as an elected deputy, and shortly after
began his work on the Committee of Public Instruction, where he set up
a revolutionary art jury, prepared for the establishment of a Central
Museum, and demanded the suppression of the Academy. Invited by
the Academy, in April of 1793, to take his regular turn as professor in
charge of the life class, he answered with ominous brevity: "I once belonged to the Academy," signing "David, Deputy of the National Convention." On August 8, 1793, he delivered the following speech before
the Convention, which immediately voted to abolish the Academy.*[35]

If there is someone among you, citizens, who must still be convinced of the absolute necessity of destroying wholesale all the Academies,
those last refuges of aristocracy, then let him give me his attention for a
moment. I promise to dispel his doubts with a few words, and to make
up his mind by appealing to his feelings. Let me demonstrate, to begin
with, what damage the Academies do to art itself, how far they are from
fulfilling the purpose which they have set themselves. Let me unmask the
party spirit which guides them, the vile jealousies of their members,
the cruel methods which they use to stifle nascent talent, and the
monkish revenge which they wreak on the persecuted student to whom,
by mischance, nature has given a talent which removes him from their
tyrannical domination. . . .

Oh, you talents lost to posterity! Great men left in neglect! I will
placate your spirits, you shall be avenged: it was your misfortune,
illustrious victims, to have lived under kings, ministers, Academicians!

I have said that I would demonstrate the damage Academies do to
the art which they profess; I shall keep my word. I shall not bore you,
citizens, with trifling details, with the bad methods of teaching used by
the Academy of Painting and Sculpture. You will be easily persuaded
when I tell you that twelve professors per year, in other words, one for
every month (and every one of them tenured), compete with one another
to destroy the fundamental principles which the young artist has received from the daily lessons of his master. Since every one of these
twelve professors approves only of his own principles (as you can well
imagine), the poor student, trying to please each one of them in turn,
must change his manner of seeing and working twelve times a year.
Having learned his art twelve times over, he ends up knowing nothing,
since he does not know what to believe. But, supposing that by some

---

[35] The text is given in J. L. Jules David, *Le peintre Louis David,* Paris, 1880,
pp. 127 ff.

rare gift from heaven he survives the poor teaching, then this child of so many fathers—on none of whom he can rely—calls down on himself the vile jealousy of all his masters who combine to ruin him. It is the policy of kings to maintain the balance of power; Academies maintain the balance of talent. Woe to the daring artist who steps across the forbidden line: he becomes an alien to the Academicians, his presence profanes the sacred, Druidical grove, and if he does not die on the spot, he is driven off by chicanery.

An example will prove my claim . . .

A young artist named Senechal, who had won the Academy's Rome Prize in sculpture, on his return to Paris lodged with a wealthy man to whose daughter he was to be married, on condition that he would be admitted to the Academy on the strength of his trial piece. Love inspires his chisel, love guides his hand; he produces a masterpiece, but so long as his teacher, so long as the Academy have not inspected it yet, he dares not to be confident of success.

Three commissioners sent by the Academy finally arrive, his master, Falconet, among them, the same Falconet who has written six fat volumes to prove that the horse of Marcus Aurelius in Rome (a recognized masterpiece of antiquity) is inferior to the one he made in Russia. . . . What were his first words? The moment this Falconet sees that the work which his pupil is about to present to the Academy impudently violates the system of the balance of talent, that it has the temerity of overstepping the line of demarcation, he tells him: "Young man, never boast of having been my pupil. Forget it, as I shall forget that I was your master. Your work makes no sense. I feel dishonored by a pupil like you."—and all this in the presence of the griefstricken girl. Tears well up in the eyes of our young man. He leaves under a pretext, he does not return. This causes some alarm. The Academicians, or rather Monsters, depart. But love is ever awake, love searches everywhere: the girl finds him at last; and where, do you suppose?—drowned in the well of her father's house.

Citizens, I could go on giving examples of this kind, but I shall remain silent, to spare your feelings.

In the name of humanity, in the name of justice for those who love art, and, above all, in the name of your love for youth: let us destroy, let us annihilate those sinister Academies. They must not be allowed to exist in the reign of liberty. Academicians, I have done my duty, now speak your sentence.

Following this speech, the painter's grandson, Jules David, reports the Convention adopted the draft of the decree which sealed the fate of the Academy of Painting and Sculpture, and which began:

First Article. All Academies and Literary Societies, licensed or endowed by the Nation, are suppressed. . . .[36]

The Academy had scarcely been abolished when it was reconstituted under the new name of Institut National. *The speed of its rebirth bears out the fact that what had prompted the destruction of the old Academy was not a fundamental hostility to the institution as such, but a determination to change its political composition. David and his followers seem never to have questioned the social utility of academic organization and academic teaching. The Convention decreed the establishment of the* Institut National *in the fall of 1795 and appointed the first members of the new body a few weeks later. David's name was included in the list. He accepted without protest.*

Joseph Anton Koch (1768–1839)

The Tirolese painter Koch exemplified "natural genius" as his generation understood it: born of poor farmers, raised in the sublime setting of the high Alps, he drew his first pictures with charred twigs on the bare rock, and seemed destined by nature to become an artist. The precocious boy received the grant of a free education at the princely Hohe Karsschule in Stuttgart, but his spirit rebelled against the school's tyrannical routines. He made a dangerous escape to Strassburg, then in the grip of the Revolution, and here had his dance round the Tree of Liberty, wearing the red Jacobin cap. When the excitement of revolution had begun to tire him, he wandered for two years among the mountains and waterfalls of the Swiss highlands. In 1794, aided by an English clergyman, he went to Rome to complete his studies. He befriended the dying Carstens (see page 108), and gradually developed a personal style of landscape painting which combined classical motifs, derived from the Carracci and Poussin, with naturalist elements. As he grew older, he became increasingly more pious and conservative and managed to be on friendly terms both with the aging pagans of his own generation and the young artists of the Nazarene brotherhood (see Vol. II, p. 32). In his polemical writings, he preserved much of his earlier radicalism and peasant earthiness. The following excerpts are taken from his Moderne Kunstchronik *and* Gedanken über ältere und neuere Malerei *which, though published as late as 1834 and 1862 respectively, were written about 1798–1820.*[37]

---

[36] The text of the decree is given in J. L. Jules David, *op. cit.,* pp. 129 ff.

[37] Cf. *Kleine Schriften* (ed. D. F. Strauss), Leipzig, 1862, pp. 303 ff., and F. H. Lehr, *Die Blütezeit Romantischer Bildkunst,* Marburg, Verlag des kunstgeschichtlichen Seminars der Universität Marburg, 1924.

On the Decadence of the Academy

Like a swarm of maggots, crawling from a rotting cheese, a countless mob of artists' crawls from the Academies. . . . In these Academies, or Schools of Art and Beauty, reigns a despotism which permits only what can be seen every day to enter into the students' brains. Mindless drawing after plaster casts and models goes on for years; the goal is not truth to nature but an abstract aesthetic mannerism which kills all character. A thousand figures drawn in this manner look as if they had all been formed in the same mould. . . . Such empty busywork is aptly named academic. . . . Many of these lighthouses of art have special composition rooms where the boys who have been tormented for six or seven years with various finger exercises could give their genius free rein —assuming that they are unlucky enough to have genius, and that this has not yet been crushed by their schooling—if they were not held in check by professors hired to keep compositional genius from kicking over its traces. . . .

The methods of study which are used in French and other European academies are quite mechanical: most painters take the merest accessories—weapons, chairs, tables, benches—from "nature." They hire carpenters and other artisans to construct models which they then color or gild; and the slavish copies which they paint after these models often look extremely realistic—as if this were of any importance. When painters of this sort have sketched their compositions, they procure sculptural models of all the figures, or sculpt such models themselves, if they can. Then they drape these dolls with garments, put them in a box which is lit through a hole at its top, and line them up in accordance with the composition. They don't draw a finger or a toe without a model. As a result, most of these painters draw correctly, often more correctly than more imaginative artists. Their details look natural, but the whole remains artificial, because it is not animated by the spirit of art. In Poussin's figures one already senses the influence of the lay-figure. His garments and their folds are usually tasteless, as in draped puppets, and the modern French school has no notion of the formation of figures other than what it derives from mannequins.

On Rococo Allegory

Now they unleashed the mythical gods and demi-gods, in addition to the allegorical virtues, to pay compliments to a tiny, effeminate despot. Hercules was made to swing his club and to proclaim that the tyrant, dozing in the arms of a mistress, was a hero. Minerva and her train of the Arts and Sciences were made to plead for protection before the potentate's bust; the Fates were encouraged to spin out the thread of his life as long as possible. Apollo, as the modern embodiment of the Day of Enlightenment, had to stop his horses in front of a bewigged head, to watch the Graces crowning and caressing it. Cerberus was not allowed to bark, Hecate was banished: only the gods of Love and the goddesses of Beauty were permitted to seat themselves on the swing of vanity. This supposedly magnificent art still fills all the aristocratic palaces dating from that period which gave to its artists such titles as *peintre du cabinet, de la cour,* and so forth.

William Blake (1757–1827)

William Blake shared with Lavater, Fuseli, Heinse, and others of the generation of Storm and Stress an extreme aversion from the Academy. Some time about 1808, he wrote into the margins of his copy of Reynolds' Discourses *a running accompaniment of protest and invective. His remarks cover the first eight* Discourses *and amount to a succinct statement of his view of art; the fact that they follow, with insistent negation, the main lines of Reynolds' argument gives them a certain coherence and progression. Blake's disagreement with Reynolds was fundamental, it stemmed from his conviction that art springs from an inborn faculty, not from acquired knowledge. The Academy therefore appeared to him as a fraud, since it pretended to teach what was in fact not teachable, and as a conspiracy designed to deprive true artists of their livelihood. Blake's annotations and other writings on art frequently have the persuasive brevity of aphorisms. They reveal him as a powerful polemicist, superior to Fuseli in this respect, and very far superior to Lavater, though he evidently borrowed from both of them.*[38]

From *Annotations to Sir Joshua Reynolds' Discourses* (c. 1808)

This man was Hired to Depress Art.
This is the Opinion of Will Blake: my Proofs of this Opinion are given in the following Notes.

*   *   *

Advice of the Popes who succeeded the Age of Raphael

Degrade first the Arts if you'd Mankind Degrade
Hire Idiots to Paint with cold light & hot shade

---

[38] The full text of the annotations, related to the pertinent passages in Reynolds' *Discourses*, is given by G. Keynes, *Poetry and Prose of William Blake*, London, Nonesuch, 1927, pp. 970 ff.

Give high Price for the worst, leave the best in disgrace,
And with Labours of Ignorance fill every place.

*   *   *

Having spent the Vigor of my Youth & Genius under Oppression of
Sr Joshua & his Gang of Cunning Hired Knaves Without Employment
& as much as could possibly be Without Bread, The Readers must Expect to Read in all my Remarks on these Books Nothing but Indigna-
tion & Resentment. While Sr Joshua was rolling in Riches, Barry was
Poor & Unemploy'd except by his own Energy; Mortimer was call'd a
Madman, & only Portrait Painting applauded & rewarded by the Rich
& Great. Reynolds & Gainsborough Blotted & Blurred one against the
other & Divided all the English World between them. Fuseli, Indignant,
almost hid himself. I am hid.

*   *   *

The Arts & Sciences are the Destruction of Tyrannies or Bad
Governments. Why should A Good Government endeavour to Depress
what is its Chief & only Support?

*   *   *

The Foundation of Empire is Art & Science. Remove them or
Degrade them, & the Empire is No More. Empire follows Art & Not
Vice Versa as Englishmen suppose.

*   *   *

To Generalize is to be an Idiot. To Particularize is the Alone Distinction of Merit. General Knowledges are those Knowledges that Idiots
possess.

*   *   *

I consider Reynolds's Discourses to the Royal Academy as the
Simulations of the Hypocrite who smiles particularly where he means to
Betray. His Praise of Raphael is like the Hysteric Smile of Revenge.
His Softness & Candour, the hidden trap & the poisoned feast. He praises
Michel Angelo for Qualities which Michel Angelo abhorr'd, & He
blames Raphael for the only Qualities which Raphael Valued. Whether
Reynolds knew what he was doing is nothing to me: the Mischief is
just the same whether a Man does it Ignorantly or Knowingly. I always
consider'd True Art & True Artists to be particularly Insulted & Degraded by the Reputation of these Discourses, As much as they were

Degraded by the Reputation of Reynolds's Paintings, & that Such Artists as Reynolds are at all times Hired by the Satans for the Depression of Art—A Pretence of Art, To destroy Art.

*   *   *

Reynolds's Opinion was that Genius May be Taught & that all Pretence to Inspiration is a Lie & a Deceit, to say the least of it. For if it is a Deceit, the whole Bible is Madness. This Opinion originates in the Greeks' Calling the Muses Daughters of Memory. The Enquiry in England is not whether a Man has Talent & Genius, But whether he is Passive & Polite & a Virtuous Ass & obedient to Noblemen's Opinions in Art & Science. If he is, he is a Good Man. If Not, he must be Starved.

*   *   *

The following annotations refer to passages in Reynolds' Discourse III *(see page 36).*

A work of Genius is a Work "Not to be obtain'd by the Invocation of Memory & her Syren Daughters, but by Devout prayer to that Eternal Spirit, who can enrich with all utterance & knowledge & sends out his Seraphim with the hallowed fire of his Altar to touch & purify the lips of whom he pleases." MILTON.

*   *   *

The following Discourse is particularly Interesting to Blockheads, as it Endeavors to prove That there is No such thing as Inspiration & that any Man of a plain Understanding may by Thieving from Others become a Mich. Angelo.

*   *   *

Without Minute Neatness of Execution The Sublime cannot Exist! Grandeur of Ideas is founded on Precision of Ideas.

*   *   *

The man who on Examining his own Mind finds nothing of Inspiration ought not to dare to be an Artist; he is a Fool & a Cunning Knave suited to the Purposes of Evil Demons.

*   *   *

The Man who never in his Mind & Thoughts travel'd to Heaven Is No Artist.

* * *

Artists who are above a plain Understanding are Mock'd & Destroy'd by this President of Fools.

* * *

What has Reasoning to do with the Art of Painting?

* * *

Knowledge of Ideal Beauty is Not to be Acquired. It is Born with us. Innate Ideas are in Every Man, Born with him; they are truly Himself.

* * *

The man who says that we have No Innate Ideas must be a Fool & Knave, Having No Con-Science or Innate Science.

* * *

One Central Form composed of all other Forms being Granted, it does not therefore follow that all other Forms are Deformity.

* * *

All Forms are Perfect in the Poet's Mind, but these are not Abstracted nor Compounded from Nature, but from Imagination.

* * *

What is General Nature, is there Such a Thing? what is General Knowledge? is there such a Thing? Strictly Speaking All Knowledge is Particular.

* * *

[In his Discourse III, *Reynolds had written (see page 43): "Albert Dürer, as Vasari has justly remarked, would, probably, have been one of the first painters of his age . . . had he been initiated into those great principles of the art which were so well understood and practiced by his contemporaries in Italy." Blake's answer strikingly recalls Wackenroder's earlier (1796) protest against this patronizing attitude toward Dürer (see Vol. II, p. 24).]*

What does this mean, *"Would have been"* one of the first Painters *of his Age?* Albert Dürer *Is,* Not would have been. Besides, let them look at Gothic Figures & Gothic Buildings & not talk of Dark Ages or of any Age. Ages are all Equal. But Genius is Always Above The Age.

*   *   *

The Two Following Discourses IV and V are Particularly Calculated for the Setting Ignorant & Vulgar Artists as Models of Execution in Art. Let him who will, follow such advice. I will not. I know that The Man's Execution is as his Conception & No better.

*   *   *

Why should Titian & The Venetians be Named in a discourse on Art? Such Idiots are not Artists.

*   *   *

A History Painter Paints The Hero, & not Man in General, but most minutely in Particular.

*   *   *

There is No Such a Thing as A Composite Style.

*   *   *

If Reynolds could not see variety of Character in Raphael, Others Can.

*   *   *

Reynolds cannot bear Expression.

*   *   *

Fresco Painting is the Most Minute. Fresco Painting is Like Miniature Painting; a Wall is a Large Ivory.

*   *   *

Reynolds Thinks that Man Learns all that he knows. I say on the Contrary that Man Brings All that he has or can have Into the World with him. Man is Born Like a Garden ready Planted & Sown. This World is too poor to produce one Seed.

*   *   *

Demonstration, Similitude & Harmony are Objects of Reasoning. Invention, Identity & Melody are Objects of Intuition.

*   *   *

God forbid that Truth should be Confined to Mathematical Demonstration!

*   *   *

Burke's Treatise on the Sublime & Beautiful is founded on the Opinions of Newton & Locke; on this Treatise Reynolds has grounded many of his assertions in all his Discourses. I read Burke's Treatise when very Young; at the same time I read Locke on Human Understanding & Bacon's Advancement of Learning; on Everyone of these Books I wrote my Opinions, & on looking them over find that my Notes on Reynolds in this Book are exactly Similar. I felt the Same Contempt & Abhorrence then that I do now. They mock Inspiration & Vision. Inspiration & Vision was then, & now is, & I hope will always Remain, my Element, my Eternal Dwelling place; how can I then hear it Contemned without returning Scorn for Scorn?

*   *   *

Rembrandt was a Generalizer. Poussin was a Particularizer.

*   *   *

Bad Pictures are always Sir Joshua's Friends.

RADICAL IDEALISM

The sense of tension which was an attribute both of revolutionary naturalism and Neoclassicism resulted from a dissonance between the social reality within which artists had to live and work and the ideal for which they strove. This produced a conflict between their interior and exterior lives which often led to severe maladjustment, and occasionally to madness. It caused artists to dissociate themselves from ordinary society and to sever their connections with institutions and patrons. Instead, they dedicated themselves to the pursuit of moral or aesthetic absolutes, to Beauty, Virtue, or Nature, substituting the goal of purity for that of social utility. Some artists attached themselves to revolutionary

*political causes, as did David; others formed ideal communities or sects;
the majority preferred to work in solitude, untainted by compromise,
conceiving vast projects without hope of realizing them. The grandiose,
cold geometry of the architectural plans of E. L. Boullée and C. N.
Ledoux in the period of 1780–1800 perfectly exemplifies this purity and
radicalism born of dissociation. The poet Friedrich Schiller (1759–1805),
in his* Letters on the Aesthetic Education of Man *(1793–1795), gave the
following description of the ideal artist:* [39]

It is true, the artist is the son of his time, but alas for him, if he
is likewise its pupil, or even favorite. Let a kind divinity snatch the
suckling betimes from his mother's breast, nourish him with the milk of
a better age, and let him come to maturity beneath a distant Grecian
sky. Then when he has become a man, let him return, a foreign shape,
into his century; not to delight it with his appearance, but terrible, like
Agamemnon's son, to purify it. He will take his material, indeed, from
the present, but borrow his form from a nobler time, nay, from beyond
all time, from the absolute, unchangeable unity of his being. Here, from
the pure ether of his divine nature, runs down the fountain of Beauty,
undefiled by the corruption of races and times, which fret far beneath
him in troubled whirlpools. Whim can dishonor his material, as it has
ennobled it, but the chaste form is removed from its vicissitudes. . . .
Humanity has lost its dignity, but art has rescued and preserved it in
significant marbles; truth survives in the midst of deception, and the
original will be restored from the copy.

But how can the artist protect himself from the corruption of his
age, which on all sides surround him? By despising its judgment. Let him
look upwards to his dignity and the law, not downwards to his prosperity
and his wants. Alike free from the vain activity, that would fain leave its
traces on the fleeting moment, and from the impatient enthusiasm, that
applies the scale of the absolute to the paltry product of time, let him
leave to the understanding, which is here at home, the sphere of the
actual; but let him strive to evolve the ideal from the union of the possible with the necessary. This let him express in fiction and truth, in the
play of his fancy and in the gravity of his deeds, in all sensible and
spiritual forms, and cast it silently into infinite time. . . .

Claude Nicolas Ledoux (1736–1806)

*The architect Ledoux sought to develop a radical new form of
architecture, combining elements of classicist style with a severe ra-*

[39] Translated by J. Weiss, in Friedrich Schiller, *Upon the Aesthetic Culture of
Man, in a Series of Letters, 1795,* Boston, 1845, Letter IX.

tionality of planning and an imaginative, symbolical use of geometric forms. Through the influence of Madame du Barry, he received several important official commissions in Paris and in the provinces, and was also named inspector of the Royal Saltworks, in which capacity he undertook the grandiose plan and partial construction of the factories at Chaux. Much more than an industrial complex, Chaux was in effect to be the blueprint for an ideal city in which the demands of social purpose, technical function, moral significance, and formal beauty were to be equally realized. Deprived of his functions in 1789, imprisoned during the Revolution, Ledoux recorded his achievements and his further ideas in a book entitled Architecture Considered from the Point of View of Art, Morality, and Legislation *of which the first and only volume appeared in 1804. The following excerpt accompanies the design for a building of extremely eccentric shape (Figure 1) which was never executed.*[40]

Workshop for the Manufacture of Hoops

All forms are contained in nature. Those which are entire give strong effects; others are the products of disordered fantasy. The Barbaric periods gave birth to monstrosities; in the more enlightened periods, fashionable errors misled the masses. Forms were often adulterated, their character denatured; false wits imagined that they could produce variety of design by playing daring tricks with details. Some used bundled columns to support the pointed vaults of our churches; others imported the filigree palaces of the East Indies; still others reproduced the corrupt and degenerate lines brought into the world by the caprice of Genius. They have deceived us, by confusing the principle with its illusory consequences.

On what firm base can we settle the inconstancy of human desire? I shall seat it on the solid throne of propriety. I shall place it on the fixed pivot round which revolves the elliptical vault. Oh, what feelings, what situations!

The artist imprints his work with the sentiments which guide him. Seeing Nature embellish its large contours, he feels that his expressive means must follow the subject which he treats, and that the expression must be unambiguous. Taste, in fact, is impartial if it is pure.

Diversity of needs will elaborate the plans and multiply the contrasts; the details contained within the design will widen the scene and place between sun and earth the shadows which will enhance it. What

[40] C. N. Ledoux, *L'architecture considérée sous le rapport de l'art, des moeurs, et de la legislation*, Paris, 1804 (reprinted 1961), I, 178 and plate 88.

Figure 1

pleasure for the eye, what advantage for education, if houses in town and country were to renounce that tedious uniformity which tires the senses of the traveller who is eager for novelty. We should then no longer see those inert surfaces which look effective only on paper because of their conventional shadings. We should then rid ourselves of Incompetence which blames its own faults on handicapping requirements. Incompetence could then no longer claim, aided by fantastic subterfuge, that it builds in deserts or on wild rocks, and that arid locations offer nothing to the imagination. It could no longer tell us that art is out of place next to gigantic nature which supplants and often crushes it. If Incompetence continued to make these excuses which show the nullity of its ideas, it would admit that it is benighted, that it sees only the darkness in the center of the flame—it would admit to us that sterility, drunk with talent, cannot rival fecundity even in the matter of mere profuseness.

One must admit, nevertheless, that a house which presents a square facade, windows and an entablature conforms more to common habits than one which is not designed according to the stereotype, but which satisfies the same needs. Everything out of the ordinary is at the mercy of the timidity which dampens the excitement of opportunity. I shall even go so far as to say that if one points out an opportunity, one risks losing it. And why should this be so? Administrators, accustomed to making excuses and to putting away plans into their portfolios, are guided by consensus. They cry out against strangeness, in order to avoid public protest. They cover their uncertainty with vacillation. Their narrow-mindedness takes fright; whatever is put up to them turns out to be too costly. They summon the uncertain architect and try to commit him to reassuring comparisons—comparisons! when shall we ever see them, so long as competition is banished and everything is done to extinguish the pure rays which flash from the dawn of Genius? The arts necessarily must regress when they are subjected to narrow principle which neutralizes ideas by aligning them with the cord of Slavery.

All in all, the construction of this building is easy and inexpensive. The workshops, situated on the ground floor, overlook the immense roads of the forest. The living quarters are raised above ground level in order to render them salubrious. The shaped voids at the center and the extremities of the building open the view on massed pine trees which correct the effects of winter, and on oaks, sycamores, and acacias which renew their foliage every spring and, by way of contrast, quieten the surfaces of the masonry. Shallow grooving extends the lines of the circles and weds them to the azure vault of the sky, of which they embrace the shape and magnificence. It may seem unimportant that a workshop seven or eight *toises* in size [one *toise* = ca 6 ft], and located in a remote forest, be impressive. But let us be true to principle. Is there anything which may not offer the eye the attractiveness of useful progress? Does anything exist which could not be electrified by art's animating breath? Certainly not! What should we say of the man who refrained from doing good because he could not trumpet his deed? What should we say? We should blame him for vain ostentation, for having an empty soul, for living in blameworthy isolation. Don't you know that often an idea which is not important in itself, which may even be bizarre, can contain the germ of excellence, so that some slight, felicitous change in it, some addition or subtraction, can make it a model for all?

If this essay can rouse feelings from apathetic slumber, if it can develop sensations which might not have arisen without this boldly conceived and executed preliminary, judge what art will have gained.

Jacques Louis David (1748–1825)

In the last decade of the 18th century, David was the only French artist of incontestably first rank; no other painter in France, with the possible exception of Prud'hon, came near him in ability. The great masters of the preceding age had died or sunk into insignificance; those who were to brighten the 19th century had not yet appeared. David's preeminence in the years of the Revolution was thus a matter of historical circumstance. The void around him was not artificial; it resulted from a pause in the sequence of generations. David's high and lonely position predestined him to play some role in the events of his time; the fact that he was attracted to power, loved the drama of public life, and had a marked talent for organization gave him an influence such as few artists have ever possessed.

Twice in his life, under Robespierre and under Napoleon, David occupied a place close to the center of political power. An ardent Jacobin, he was elected Deputy to the Convention in September of 1792, presided over this body during January of 1793, and cast his vote for the execution of Louis XVI. At the height of the Terror, he served as the leading member of the Committee of Public Instruction. In this latter position, he was relentlessly active: his share in the abolition of the Academy has already been noted (page 115); he helped, in addition, to develop a grandiose project for the embellishment of Paris, set up a National Jury of the Arts, organized the Central Museum (see Vol. II, p. 4), voted credits for the purchase of paintings by Rubens and Poussin, and designed the uniforms of the Republican functionaries. Although he did not bear the title, he was in fact the minister of art in the revolutionary government; more than that, he served as the official representative of the world of art in the councils of the Revolution and acted as impressario of the immense public pageants which were the Revolution's most original device for the political indoctrination of the masses. As an orator and propagandist, David carried the classicist style to an extreme which he avoided in his painting. His Cyclopean improvisations recall the fantasies of such architects of the period as Ledoux and Boullée. But he was an intensely practical man; his fantasies tended toward concrete ends. He applied the suggestions of style and the language of symbols not to aesthetic but to political purposes. Because of its very nature, much of David's work for the Revolution remained ephemeral; its influence, nevertheless, was deep. His designs for the Republican festivals realized, more completely than work in the more conventional media could have

*done, the special possibilities which lay in neoclassicism. They seemed
to portend the long-awaited regeneration of art through a return to significant content and popular function.*

*David exercised his leadership through practical example and pub-
lic attitude. Instinct had a large share in his art and his politics. As a
theoretician he was insignificant. He reacted strongly and emotionally
to concrete situations, and though he was inclined to rationalize, he
lacked firm principle. This helps to explain the inconsistencies in his
conduct, the shifts in style and in political allegiance (see Vol. II, p. 15),
which some have blamed, unjustly, on a weakness of character.*

David Designs the Republican Uniform (1792)

*The Scottish physician John Moore (1729–1802), a resident in Paris
during the early part of the Revolution, reports:* [41]

David, the celebrated painter, who is a Member of the Convention
and a zealous Republican, has sketched some designs for a republican
dress, which he seems eager to have introduced; it resembles the old
Spanish dress, consisting of a jacket with tight trowsers, a coat without
sleeves above the jacket, a short cloak, which may either hang loose from
the left shoulder or be drawn over both: a belt to which two pistols and
a sword may be attached, a round hat and feather, are also part of this
dress, according to the sketches of David; in which full as much attention
is paid to picturesque effect as to conveniency. This artist is using all
his influence, I understand, to engage his friends to adopt it, and is in
hopes that the Municipality of Paris will appear in it at a public feast,
or rejoicing, which is expected soon. I said to the person who gave me
this account, "that I was surprised that David, who was so great a
patriot, should be so anxious about an object of this kind."

He answered, "that David had been a painter before he was a
patriot."

Part of this dress is already adopted by many; but I have only seen
one person in public completely equipped with the whole; and as he
had managed it, his appearance was rather fantastical. His jacket and
trowsers were blue; his coat, through which the blue sleeves appeared,
was white with a scarlet cape; his round hat was amply supplied with
plumage; he had two pistols stuck in his belt, and a very formidable
sabre at his side: he is a tall man, and of a very warlike figure; I took
him for a Major of Dragoons at least. On enquiry I find he is a miniature
painter.

[41] John Moore, *A Journal during a Residence in France,* London, 1793, II, 433.

David Undertakes the Training of Two Youths Whom Nature has Destined for Art

On January 14, 1792, a Deputy from the Department du Drone presented to the National Assembly the twin brothers Joseph and Pierre Franque, simple shepherds, who had shown a precocious, natural gift for art. In their native mountains, the children had carved stones, engraved human figures, and drawn landscapes. When they were offered an education at the expense of the Department du Drone, it became evident that there was no teacher in the district who was capable of instructing them. Representative Dumas moved in the National Assembly that the twins be handed over to David for the completion of their training. This proposal was adopted. Shortly thereafter, the Moniteur Universel *of February 9, 1792, published the following letter by the artist:* [42]

Mr. President: I have been asked by the Assembly to teach the principles of art to two children whom Nature seems to have destined to be painters, but to whom Chance has denied the means for acquiring the necessary knowledge. I am overjoyed to be chosen to be the first teacher of these youths who could be called Children of the Nation, since they owe everything to her. Let me say again: I am overjoyed. My heart feels this joy, I cannot express it well in words, since my art consists of deeds, not words. Give me but a little time, and my assiduous care will prove how highly I value the honor of having been chosen. This will be my prize. I do not suppose that the Assembly will want to lessen the honor it has shown me, by offering a salary for the care which I shall give to the instruction of these adopted children. The love of money has never penetrated into my heart, to affect that love of glory which I value above all.

[signed]   David.

David Commemorates the Martyrs of the Revolution

On January 20, 1793, Michel Lepelletier de Saint-Fargeau, a member of the Convention who, like David, had voted for the death of Louis XVI, was assassinated by a former officer of the guards. The Convention voted him the honors of the Pantheon. On March 29th, David presented his painting of the dead Lepelletier to the Convention. This work, now lost, was the first of his three commemorative portraits of martyrs of the

---

[42] J. L. Jules David, *Le peintre Louis David*, Paris, 1880, p. 139.

Revolution, the other two being the portraits of Marat and of Barra. The following is the text of David's presentation speech: [43]

Citizens-Representatives,

Every one of us is accountable to his country for the talents which he has received from Nature. Though these may differ in kind, their aim must be the same for all. True patriots should eagerly seize every opportunity for enlightening their fellow citizens and for presenting to them sublime examples of heroism and virtue.

This I have tried to do in offering to the National Convention my painting of Michel Lepelletier who was slain by cowards for having voted the Tyrant's death.

Citizens, the Supreme Being who distributes His gifts among all His children has decreed that I should express my sentiments and thoughts through the medium of painting, rather than through that sublime voice of eloquence which is raised among us here by the Children of Liberty. Respectfully heeding His immutable decree, I remain silent, but I shall have fulfilled my task if my picture will some day cause an aged father to speak thus to.his numerous family assembled around him: "Come, children, look at the Representative who was the first to die in order that you might have Liberty. Look at his features: how serene they are! It is because those who die for their country die blameless. Do you see that sword hanging over his head, suspended by a single hair? This, dear children, is to show how much courage it took for Michel Lepelletier and his generous colleagues to send to the scaffold the infamous Tyrant who had so long been our oppressor: for at the slightest movement, this hair might break and all would die! Do you see the deep wound? . . . Are you crying, children, and turning your faces away? But look at this wreath, it signifies Immortality. The Fatherland holds it in readiness for each of its children; learn to be worthy of it, the occasions will not be wanting for those of great soul. If Ambition ever whispers to you of dictators, tribunes, and arbiters, or tries to usurp the smallest particle of the people's sovereignty, or if Cowardice should propose a king—then fight, or die like Michel Lepelletier, rather than consent. The laurel wreath of Immortality, my children, will then be your reward."

I beg the Convention to accept this homage of my feeble talent; should you deign to receive it, I will consider myself richly rewarded.

After the assassination of Marat, on July 13, 1793, David was again called upon to exercise his patriotic talent. His pupil and biographer, Etienne Delécluze, gives the following description of the event: [44]

[43] David, *op. cit.*, p. 150.
[44] David, *op. cit.*, p. 155.

The day after the assassination of Marat, the anniversary of the 14th of July, a deputation presented itself before the Convention to express the people's sorrow. Its spokesman, a certain Guirault, said: "Oh, shameful crime! a patricidal hand has struck down the most fearless defender of the people. He had dedicated himself to Liberty. Our eyes still search for him among you, Representatives! Oh, horrible spectacle! he lies on his death bed. Where are you, David? You have given to posterity the image of Lepelletier dying for his country. There is still another picture for you to do. . . ."

"Yes, I shall do it," cried David, deeply moved.

David's Project for the Immortalization of Barra and Viala (July 28, 1794)

This was the last of the revolutionary ceremonies planned by David. It was never carried out. Robespierre fell, one day before it was to be held. David himself was accused and imprisoned; he narrowly missed accompanying the Jacobin leaders to the guillotine on the very day for which this celebration had been planned. The previous patriotic spectacle organized by David, and the last to be realized, the Feast of the Supreme Being (June 8, 1794), had cast Robespierre in the role of high priest— a circumstance which possibly hastened his downfall.

Barra and Viala, the heroes who were to have been commemorated in the projected ceremonies were youths, still in their teens, who had been killed in the civil war in the Vendée. David had begun a painting of the death of Barra; the fall of the Jacobins prevented its completion. The following excerpts are taken from David's plans for the ceremonies, for which he sought, and received, the Convention's formal approval: [45]

At three o'clock in the afternoon, an artillery salvo discharged from the Eastern end of the Ile de la Cité announces the beginning of the ceremonies.

The people immediately assemble in the Jardin National; the members of the Convention make their entry into the amphitheater, attired in their official garb as Representatives of the People. Each member carries in his hands the symbol of his mission. They are preceded by a military band. The musicians chant a refrain suitable to the occasion.

At the conclusion of this song, the President of the Convention ascends the tribune and delivers a speech in which he describes to the people the heroic traits of Barra and Agricol Viala, their filial piety, and, in short, the reasons for which they have been accorded the honors of the Pantheon. He then hands over the urn containing Viala's ashes to

[45] David, *op. cit.,* p. 214.

the deputation of children, selected from all the Sections of Paris and of the same age as our young Republicans, i.e., between eleven and thirteen years.

The mortal remains of Barra, contained in the other urn, are to be handed over to the mothers whose children have died gloriously in defense of our Liberty. . . .

At precisely five o'clock, a second artillery salvo is heard. The deputations of mothers and children begin to march, divided into two columns. The procession is preceded by a large contingent of drummers, the lugubrious and majestic sounds of whose instruments express the surging emotion of a great people assembled for the most august of ceremonies.

Each column is to be headed by paintings of Barra and Viala representing their actions. . . . The column on the right will consist of the deputations of children, that on the left of the deputations of mothers. The space between the columns will be occupied by theatrical performers, arranged in six groups, in the following order: the first group is to consist of instrumental musicians, the second of singers, the third of male dancers, the fourth of female singers, the fifth of female dancers, the sixth of poets who will recite verses composed by them in honor of the young heroes.

Next follow the Representatives of the People, surrounded by brave soldiers who have been wounded in the defense of their country. The President of the Convention gives his right hand to one of them, who has been chosen by lot, his left hand to the mother of Barra and her daughters. The masses of the people close the march.

From time to time, the drummers will sound a funereal drum roll, and the band will play a mournful tune. The singers will express our grief with plaintive melodies, the dancers with lugubrious or martial pantomime.

The columns come to a halt. There is complete silence. Suddenly, all the people raise their voices in unison, to cry three times: "They have died for their country."

On arriving at the Pantheon, the two columns will group themselves in a wide half-circle, in such a way as to leave a passage between them for the members of the Convention who will station themselves on the steps of the Temple. The children, musicians, singers, dancers, and poets will stand on the side of Viala, the mothers, and the women singers and dancers on the side of Barra.

In the meantime, the two urns are to be placed on an altar in the center of the square. Round this altar, the young dancers will perform a funeral dance expressive of deepest grief; they will scatter cypress branches on the urns. At the same time, the musicians and the singers will mourn, with their music, the ravages of fanaticism which have deprived us of these young Republicans.

Renewed silence follows the cries of grief. The President of the Convention steps forward, kisses the urns, and, raising his eyes to the heavens, bestows the honor of immortality on Barra and Agricol Viala in the presence of the Supreme Being and of the people. In the name of the grateful Fatherland, he places them in the Pantheon, the doors of which open at this instant.

Suddenly, the scene changes. Grief is replaced by public rejoicing, and the people, three times over raise the shout: "They are immortal!"

The great bells toll, and the games begin.

The drummers beat out a warlike rhythm, the female dancers execute a joyous step, scattering flowers on the urn, causing the cypress branches to become invisible. The male dancers strike martial attitudes to the accompaniment of the music, celebrating the glory of the heroes, and the soldiers go through military manoeuvres. . . .

The President closes the doors of the Temple and gives the signal for the departure. . . .

The Sect of the "Primitifs"

During the late 1790's, while working on the Battle of Romans and Sabines *(see page 111), David strove for a purer, more "Greek" style than he had achieved in his earlier classicist compositions. The severity and simplicity of early Greek art particularly appealed to him, and in drawing the attention of his pupils to the beauties of archaic style, he made them aware of similar qualities in the "primitive" work of Giotto, Fra Angelico, and Perugino. Several of his pupils of that time seized on his suggestion and exaggerated it to the point of caricature. Known variously as* Barbus *("Beards"),* Penseurs, *or* Primitifs, *these young artists, not content with introducing archaisms into their work, were determined to apply the ethic of extreme simplicity and purity to their daily conduct and appearance. They seem to have produced little, but the character and aim of their association is of some interest. Their artistic program marks a radicalization of neoclassicism to the point of near-abstraction. Their social eccentricity illustrates a tendency, fairly widespread at the time, toward the formation of Utopian brotherhoods or quasi-monastic communities. The following account of the* Primitifs *was written by the painter Etienne Delécluze (1781–1863), their colleague and contemporary in the studio of David.*[46] *It was composed in 1832, and carries a polemical*

---

46 E. Delécluze, *Louis David, son école et son temps,* Paris, 1855, pp. 420 ff. Delécluze's article had originally appeared in *Le Livre des Cent-et-Un,* a miscellany published by Ladvocat, Paris, 1832, VII, 61. Cf. also G. Levitine, "The Primitifs and their Critics in the Year 1800," *Studies in Romanticism,* Boston University, I (Summer 1962), No. 4, p. 209.

point, directed against the Jeunes France, *the Bohemians of a later generation, who bore a superficial resemblance to the* Primitifs. *(Frances Trollope described them as having "long and matted locks that hang in heavy, ominous dirtiness. . . . The throat is bare, at least from linen; but a plentiful and very disgusting profusion of hair supplies its place.")* [47]

I have known two generations of bearded friends, the first from 1799 to 1803, the second, if I remember correctly, from 1827 until this present year of 1832. . . .

It is well known that the revolution in the arts and in the study of classical antiquity which swept Europe preceded, by a few years, the great political Revolution in France. Heyne's and Winckelmann's searching studies of the writings and monuments of antiquity had restored the prestige of the Greeks and Romans. We can assume that this predisposed the political revolutionaries of 1789 to try to govern, and even to clothe, us in the manner of the Spartans and Romans. Whatever the actual reason, the fact remains that the craze for imitating the Ancients took hold of the most energetic and active minds, if not necessarily the best. The pictorial arts, theater, literature, and even household furnishings were influenced by this mania for copying the Romans, followed by the craze for imitating the Greeks. It was shortly after the Terror that Greek vases of the type called "Etruscan" became better known to artists, and it was precisely in this period that there arose the taste for Greek forms and ornament in women's fashions and in the decoration of interiors, down to the most ordinary utensils.

My earliest bearded friends were of this time. Until then, they had shaved and dressed like everyone else. But the moment arrived when David, whose pupils they were like myself, exhibited his picture of the *Battle of the Romans and Sabines.* Although this painting won the admiration of the public, it did not receive the wholehearted approval of some of the master's disciples. At first, these youngsters hazarded only slight criticisms. Gradually, they became more severe, and finally decided that, despite a few praiseworthy attempts to follow Greek models, the painting contained nothing of the simplicity, grandeur, or primitiveness —this last being the key term—which are to be found in Greek vase painting; and immediately these heretical pupils started calling David Van Loo, Pompadour, and Rococo. . . .

David could not tolerate such criticisms, particularly from his own students. Without making a scene, he found ways of telling those who no longer agreed with his teaching that they should stop disturbing the studies of their former colleagues. •

It was then that they formed the sect which was to be called the "Thinkers" or "Primitives." Without defining, for the time being, the odd

[47] Frances Trollope, *Paris and the Parisians in 1835,* New York, 1836, p. 124.

principles which they intended to follow in their painting, they agreed to adopt the Greek costume, and particularly that of the archaic Greeks, in order to preserve themselves from the mannered and hypocritical ways of modern society. To them, Pericles was just another Louis XIV, living in a century already tinged with decadence. In short, they modelled their clothes after those worn by the figures on Sicilian vases, believed to be the most ancient of all, and let their hair and beards grow.

There were only a few, about five or six, who had the will and the means to indulge in this caprice, but they made quite a stir. There must still be some people in Paris who remember having seen two bearded young men walking the streets around 1799, the one dressed like Agamemnon, the other like Paris in his Phrygian robe. Although I was friends with both of them, I was closer to Agamemnon who visited me fairly often, to the great amazement of the porter and my neighbors.

Agamemnon was about twenty years old at that time. He was tall and thin, with bushy hair and beard; his eye was fiery, and he wore an expression which was both passionate and kind and which made him seem imposing, and at the same time attractive. There was something about him which reminded one of Mohammed and of Christ, both of whom he deeply revered. He was keen-witted and had an easy, copious and graceful eloquence. . . . As for his costume, it was quite simple, consisting of a large tunic which reached down to his ankles and a voluminous cloak which he would draw over his head in times of rain or sun. I have seen few actors, not even excepting Talma, who wore this kind of costume with greater ease and grace than my friend Agamemnon. . . .

I saw him only once or twice in his studio, an enormous room cut diagonally by a canvas thirty feet long. In the dark triangle behind the canvas were the straw on which he slept and a few household articles; the other triangle constituted the studio proper. There I watched my friend Agamemnon preparing his palette which measured four feet across, working on his canvas on which he had begun to draw the subject of Patroclus sending Briseis back to Agamemnon, the king of kings. . . .

It was his opinion that, in order to put an end to harmful doctrines and prevent the spread of false taste, only three or four statues from the museum of classical art should be preserved, and he advocated setting fire to the picture gallery, after removal of no more than a dozen works. The basic tenet of his system was to study classical art and to work only from nature. But he looked on imitation as a very subordinate means of art, and on sublime beauty as art's true and only aim. . . .

His literary tastes were every bit as exclusive as his artistic doctrines. Just as in Greek art he valued only the vase paintings, statues and reliefs of the most archaic style, so he found genuine, substantial and indisputable worth only in the Bible and the poems of Homer and

Ossian. He related everything to these three eminences, and gave attention to other writings only when they reflected these three monuments of literature. Agamemnon had overcome the disadvantage of a neglected education through discriminating and intensive reading. He was well versed in the Old and New Testament; he had read, besides translations of Homer, nearly all Greek writers of the best period; and he had practically memorized the French translation of Ossian's poems. . . .

At that time, no one doubted their authenticity. Some people, like my friend Agamemnon, found them sublime and admirable; others found them monotonous and occasionally boring. I was of this latter opinion. Having quoted abundantly from the poems of Fingal. . . . He told me with the grave authority and fervor of a prophet: "Homer is admirable, but Genesis, the story of Joseph, Job, Ecclesiastes, and the Gospels are far superior to Homer, no doubt about that. But I assure you," he added with rising emphasis, "that Ossian's grandeur surpasses all of them, and for this reason: he is truer and, mark my words, more *primitive!*" . . . My perplexity only heightened my friend Agamemnon's assurance; wrapped in his cloak and stroking his long beard, he seemed to be focusing all his reflections on one point, to reduce them to a single thought and one concise and firm sentence—"Homer? Ossian?" he asked himself, "the sun? the moon? That's the question. Actually, I think I prefer the moon; it is simpler, more noble, more *primitive!*"

Such were, more or less, the opinions and sayings of the grand master of the bearded men of Paris in the last years of the eighteenth century. . . .

The sect of the "Thinkers" or "Primitives" was the forward edge of the society of that time, the time of the Directory and Consulate. After the end of the Terror, the taste for ancient art had temporarily displaced the religious sentiments and the social or literary distractions which had occupied the souls and minds of people prior to the revolution. France was treating herself to a show of paganism. All classes of society mingled at the theater and other pleasure haunts. In the parks, women dressed in the Greek manner displayed the grace and beauty of their forms to public admiration. All the young men, rich and poor alike, daily exposed their naked bodies along the banks of the Seine, and tested their strength and skill in swimming. Athletic contests were held in the Bois de Boulogne on summer evenings; on holidays, there were foot races, horse races, and chariot races in the Champ de Mars, all in the Greek style. At civic ceremonies, one observed high priests reminiscent of Chalchas and maidens like those of the Parthenon frieze; and more than once I have come across sacrificial offerings of pitch-pine, substituting for incense, burning on the lawns of the Champs Elysées before pasteboard replicas of the temples of Paestum. In those days, all classes of society mingled, walked, laughed, and danced together under the auspices of the only true aristocracy then recognized in France, beauty.

The story of the beard of my friend Agamemnon is, in effect, a concise summary of the time in which this young man lived, for he died young, and his end coincided with the end of the saturnalia of the Directory.

After Agamemnon's death, all the members of his sect shaved their beards, put on their hose and shabby jackets. Bonaparte had already arrived on the scene with sword and tri-cornered hat.

Revolutionary Vandalism

The wholesale destruction of works of art which occurred during the French Revolution resulted partly from neglect or pillage, partly from deliberate political action. The revolutionary leaders regarded works of art as public symbols: palace and church in their view stood for tyranny and priestcraft, and therefore seemed the proper targets for popular vengeance. Monuments in the Gothic style particularly stirred the wrath of patriots, because they recalled the days of feudalism. Cathedrals suffered execution, like kings, in symbolical punishment for ancient crimes.

Large-scale destruction of religious and monarchical monuments began in 1792. During August of that year, the Scottish physician John Moore (1729–1802) reported from Paris: [48]

Above the great gate of the church of Notre Dame, are the figures in stone of twenty-six Kings of France, from Childebert the First to Philip August. I was told that in this general fury against kings, all those venerable personages had been hewn to pieces by the people. I had the curiosity to go to the cathedral on purpose, to see whether absurd zeal had been carried this length, and had the satisfaction of finding this royal society safe and uninjured by any hand but that of Time.

The ridiculous gigantic statue of St. Christopher, with the Bon Dieu upon his shoulders, which I remember to have stood formerly within the church, is now removed; but I believe the revolution cannot claim the merit of this improvement, as it was made before it began.

Not long after, in September of 1792, Moore was able to observe actual vandalism at Chantilly: [49]

A party of national guards, detached by order of the Commune de Paris, has been here; they only left Chantilly this morning: they carried

48 John Moore, *op. cit.,* I, p. 85.
49 John Moore, *op. cit.,* I, p. 325.

with them, in waggons, a vast quantity of stuff proper for soldiers' tents which was in this place. A party which was here some time ago, but since the 10th of August, carried away all the horses of every kind which remained in the stables, also a statue of Louis XIV which was within the castle. They also overset and broke in pieces the fine figures which ornamented the front of the magnificent stables: they treated in the same manner the equestrian statue of Henry de Montmorency, Constable of France in the time of Henry IV. The materials of those, being metal, were carried by the same party in waggons to Paris. They had the brutality, before they set out, to knock off the head of the beautiful pedestrian statue of the Great Condé, which stood in the grand staircase of the castle.

David Proposes a Monument to the French People (1793)

On November 7, 1793, Louis David (see pages 111, 115 and 130)
proposed to the Convention that the debris of royal monuments be put
to patriotic use: [50]

Unable to usurp God's place in the churches, the kings took possession of their portals. Here they put their effigies, no doubt so that the people's adoration should come to a stop at the entrance of the sanctuary. Accustomed to laying their hands on everything, they had the presumption of competing with God Himself for the incense which men offered Him. You have overthrown these insolent usurpers; laughed to scorn, they now litter the soil which they once stained with their crimes.

Let a monument be raised within the confines of the Commune of Paris, close to the church which the kings once made their Pantheon, to be a reminder to our descendants and the first trophy erected by the Sovereign People in its victory over the tyrants. Let the dismembered fragments of these statues form a lasting monument of the kings' downfall and the people's glory. Let the traveler who passes through this reborn country take back to his homeland the useful lesson: "Once I saw kings in Paris; when I returned, they were no more." (Applause.)

I propose, therefore, that a monument be erected in the square of the Pont Neuf. It is to represent the Giant People, the People of France.

Let this statue, imposing in its strength and simplicity, be inscribed in large letters, on the forehead: *Light;* on the chest: *Nature* and *Truth;* on the arms: *Strength, Courage.* Put in one of its hands the statues of Liberty and Equality embracing one another and ready to traverse the world, in order to show that they are founded on the genius and virtue

[50] E. Delécluze, *op. cit.*, p. 156.

of the people. And let this statue of the people stand upright and hold in its other hand that terrible club with which the ancients armed their Hercules.

It is up to us to raise such a monument. Other peoples who loved liberty have raised similar ones before us. Not far from our borders lie the bones of the tyrants' slaves who attacked the liberty of the Swiss. Piled into pyramids, they now threaten those impudent kings who would dare to desecrate the land of free men.

Thus we shall pile up in Paris the effigies of the kings and their vile attributes, to serve as the pedestal for the emblem of the French people.

David's suggestion did not go unheeded. At the following Salon (1795), the sculptor C. Dumont exhibited the model for a colossal statue of The Victorious French People, Presenting Liberty and Equality.

Method for the Destruction of Gothic Churches (1800)

At the Salon of 1800, an architect by the name of Petit Radel, Inspector-General of Civil Structures, exhibited a design which the official catalogue describes as follows: [51]

516. DESTRUCTION OF A CHURCH IN THE GOTHIC STYLE, BY MEANS OF FIRE

In order to minimize the dangers which this kind of operation entails, the piers are to be hollowed, near their bases, at a height of two stone courses. As stones are removed, half their volume is replaced by dry wood. This is continued throughout. Kindling is then inserted, and fire set to the wood. When enough of the wood has burned, it gives way under the weight of the masonry, and the whole structure collapses in less than ten minutes.

NEW IMAGES AND SYMBOLS

The translation of pure thought into picture was a particular problem for certain artists of the period around 1800 whose ideas were too unfamiliar, complex, or abstract to be cast into conventional forms. Two main possibilities were open to them: an indirect expression of their thought through the medium of traditional kinds of images, or a direct

[51] *Explication des ouvrages de peinture et dessins . . . exposés au Musée Central des Arts*, Paris, 1800, p. 82.

expression through new images. Most artists, understandably, preferred to express themselves with the help of subjects, symbols, and stylistic devices taken from tradition. David, for example, often used classical history or myth to deliver comments on the political reality of his time. His painting of the Battle of Romans and Sabines *(see page 111) was meant to symbolize the need for reconciliation after fratricidal conflict, its classical style and subject were the vehicle for a specific, modern meaning. But there were other artists who believed that idea and image could not be considered separately, and who felt that every idea demanded its own, particular form. To express themselves, they attempted to devise a personal pictorial language, either by recomposing elements from traditional iconography into new configurations, or by fusing thought and image in one spontaneous vision.*

Philipp Otto Runge (1777–1810)

The painter Runge was born in the North German harbor town of Wolgast, the son of a merchant and ship builder. He grew up among relatives and friends who combined a strong Protestant piety with a wide-ranging interest in literature and philosophical speculation. After two unsatisfactory years at the Academy in Copenhagen (1799–1801), spent in submission to the routines of neoclassical pedagogy, he went to Dresden which was then a main center of the young Romantic movement, to train himself further through independent study. He met Ludwig Tieck, the friend of Wackenroder and Friedrich Schlegel (see Vol. II, pp. 18, 28), whose writings he already knew. Tieck introduced him to the mystical teachings of Jakob Boehme which were to influence the symbolism of his work, in much the same way in which they had influenced the thought and work of William Blake.

Runge's letters of this time (1801–1802) show him on the verge of a great decision. Although he had not yet produced any significant, original work, he felt strong enough not only to shake off academic conventions, but to undertake the creation of a wholly new kind of art. He had in mind an art of personal revelation which would express with compelling force and clarity his own, scarcely utterable intimations of God, and of the workings of God in nature and in the human soul. For this he needed a new pictorial language. Unlike the retrospective romantics (see Vol. II, p. 32) who bowed to the authority of Catholic traditions and savored the sweet severity of archaic style, the Protestant Runge believed that the spirit and form of earlier art were dead. The new religion could not be expressed in the old hieroglyphics. What past art had given only at second hand, through descriptive representation and borrowed subject matter, Runge, with incredible boldness, resolved to express directly, through symbolical imagery and meaningful color. Runge's conception of art as a form of language recalls Wackenroder (see Vol. II, p. 25), but while Wackenroder thought of art as one of the "miraculous languages" spoken by God, Runge sought for an art of unlimited communication between human beings. He gave the name of landscape *to the art which he envisioned, to distinguish it from history painting, but the works in which he tried to realize his idea were actually figurative allegories placed in settings which either approached conventional landscape, like the sky and meadow of his* Morning, *or verged on abstract pattern, like the floral arabesques of his drawings of the* Times of Day.

The special difficulty which confronts the kind of expression which Runge attempted is that it must convey, through relatively simple forms, the very complex experience to which Runge always referred only as "feeling," though he evidently had in mind philosophical or religious insights imbedded in a current of strong emotion. His approach to the solution of the problem was partly intuitive, partly methodical, and even scientific, as in his elaborate researches into color which won him Goethe's respect. He failed to achieve in his work the complete unity of form and spirit which his idea demanded. His symbols struck contemporaries as obscure (see Vol. II, p. 31). At the time of his very early death, his painting was still a patchwork of allegory and portrait, realist detail and abstract arrangement, expressive color and classicist contour. But the profundity and daring of his conception of art place him, with Blake who was his closest intellectual relative, among the most original minds of his time.

Runge's writings, including the letters from which the following excerpts are taken, were published in 1840 by his brother Daniel who tried to smoothe Runge's difficult language, but let stand many tangled sentences which resist exact translation.[52]

[1801]

Since my youth, I have often longed to convey to others, through words, signs, or whatever else might serve, something of the feeling which in my best hours animates me with a serene and stirring life. I thought: even if no one really cares about your feeling, there must be another who shares it. And if one could tell the other of it, this emotion of our soul should become as palpable as a handshake and a glance. I valued the thought more than laborious learning, since it seemed to me that this was, after all, the actual aim of science and art. But I found few people who understood me. In the beginning, I thought that people

52 *Hinterlassene Schriften von Philipp Otto Runge,* edited by Daniel Runge, Hamburg, 1840, I, 3 ff. (letter of 1801); 5 ff. (letter of February 1802); 7 ff. (letter of March 7, 1802); 16 ff. (letter of November 7, 1802). See also Gunnar Berefelt, *Philipp Otto Runge, zwischen Aufbruch und Opposition, 1777–1802,* Uppsala, Almquist and Wiksell, 1961.

really did understand, but pretended not to, for fear of seeming childish. Then I found that they really did not want to be children. . . . Several years ago, I discovered that there exist certain words through which men can deeply understand one another. But these words have nearly passed out of use; only their letters are preserved, as rare curiosities. People sometimes imitated and rearranged them, since they had heard that, long ago, these letters had been writing, which made them wonder whether the signs could still yield a sound. The secret lay evidently not in mere arrangement. When they opened the Egyptian tombs and found them full of hieroglyphics, people complained that these were incomprehensible. I was not surprised. What is the use of tombs, if not to bury all, the spirit as well as the living form of the hieroglyphics? And is it really certain that we understand the paintings of the Italian masters? It seems to me that people want only to understand the letters, not the words which they form. Many have in time become writers who simply like lettering —a thing which makes as much sense as a copy clerk promoted to a minister of state, simply because of his ability to make clean copies of decrees. . . .

I concluded that true art consisted of expression . . . but it needs something to express. The living force which created heaven and earth, and of which our living soul is the image, must stir and move and flourish in us, so that we may discover how much love there is in ourselves and all around us. Once we come to see and believe it, this hidden love will be found to gaze at us benevolently from every flower and color, from behind every fence and shrub, from behind the clouds and the most distant stars. I think that it must be a great joy to find a language within ourselves to express this feeling, even if only for family talk. How good to live in a family in which one can converse in this language, only fools would not enjoy it. I think that the Apostles, the great musicians, the great poets and painters really wanted to form such a family. The Apostles did succeed in this, the others only in part. . . .

[February 1802]

Art of all periods teaches us that humanity changes, and that a period, once past, never returns. Whatever gave us the disastrous idea of trying to bring back the art of the past? In Egyptian art, we see the hard, iron roughness of the human race. The Greeks deeply felt their religion, and it dissolved into works of art. Michelangelo marked the highest point in the development of composition; in the *Last Judgment* historical composition reached its final limits. Raphael already painted many compositions which can no longer be called purely historical. The *Sistine Madonna* in Dresden is clearly only a state of feeling, expressed in the form of a familiar figure. And since Raphael's time, there has been no true history painting. All beautiful compositions now tend toward landscape, so, for instance, Guido Reni's *Aurora*. But until now no landscape artist has given his landscapes a true significance, or endowed them with allegorical meaning and intelligible, beautiful ideas. But don't we all see spirits in the clouds at sunset? Doesn't this inspire quite definite thoughts in our soul? Is it not true that a work of art comes into being only at the moment when we feel ourselves united with the universe? Can't I capture the vanishing moon, as I might capture a vanishing figure which has awakened a thought in me, and couldn't both, moon or figure, become art? And what artist who had really sensed this, and who had been awakened by nature (which we see clearly only in ourselves, in our love, and in the sky) could fail to seize the right subject for the expression of his feeling? How could he possibly lack a subject? . . . What is the use of reviving old art? The Greeks carried formal and bodily beauty to its highest point at a time when their gods were declining. The artists of modern Rome went farthest in the development of historical painting at a time when the Catholic faith was perishing. In our time, too, something is about to die. We stand on the brink of all the religions which have come down from the Catholic. The abstractions are fading away: everything is becoming more airy and light than before, everything gravitates toward landscape. The artists search for something definite in this vagueness and do not know where to start. Some, mistakenly, go back into history, and become confused. But could we not reach the point of highest perfection in a new kind of art, in this art of landscape, and perhaps reach a higher beauty than existed before? I want to express my life in a series of works; when the sun sets and the moon gilds the clouds, I shall capture the fugitive spirits. Perhaps we shall not live to see the day of this art's full beauty, but we will devote our life to its fulfillment. No common thought shall enter our soul. We can attain this high level of beauty only if we cherish the beautiful and good with fervent love. We must become children again to reach perfection.

[To his brother Daniel, March 9, 1802]

I once reflected on how the world might be overturned by a war, and on how such a war might come about, for I saw no other way. But war has turned into a science, and real war has ceased—there is no nation now which could massacre all of Europe and the civilized world, as the Germans once massacred the Romans when that nation had lost its vitality. In other words, I could see no other way than a general Judgment Day on which the earth would open up to devour the whole human race, leaving no trace of humanity's achievements up to the present day.

These thoughts were prompted by some melancholy remarks which Tieck made recently when he was ill, remarks about the spread of culture which led to the notion of a Judgment Day. And I began to reflect on how this high culture of ours cannot be brought to its senses, except by such extreme means . . . And it seemed evident to me that, after art had reached the peak of its development in a given period (after the Olympian Zeus was carved, or the *Last Judgment* painted), it always went into a decline and dissolved, in order to reach out again toward another, perhaps even more beautiful stage of development. And I asked myself: are we now on the point of burying such a period?

I was lost in amazement, I could think no further. I sat down before my picture, and all my earlier thoughts about it passed through my soul. I thought about its growth, about the feelings which always overcome me when I see the moon or the setting sun, about the divination of spirits, and the destruction of the world.

When the sky above me teems with stars, when the wind blows through the vastness of space, and the wave breaks in the immense night; when above the forest the reddish morning light appears, and the sun begins to illuminate the world; when the valley steams, and I lie tossing in the grass which sparkles with dew; when every leaf and blade of grass teems with life, and the earth comes to life and stirs beneath me, and everything harmonizes in one great chord: then my soul rejoices and soars in the immeasurable space around me. There is no high or low, no time, no beginning or end. I hear and feel the living breath of God Who holds and supports the world, in Whom everything lives and acts—this is our highest feeling: God.

The deepest awareness in our soul—that there is a God above us; that everything once came into being, existed, and perished; that everything is now coming into being, existing, and perishing all around us; that in time everything will come into being, will exist, and will perish again; that there is no rest, no standing still; that the living soul within us came from Him and will return to Him, and will continue to exist when heaven and earth are no more—this is the clearest and most certain awareness of our self and our eternity.

We sense that something mercilessly severe and terrifyingly eternal confronts a sweet, everlasting, boundless love in furious conflict, comparable to the contrast between hard and soft, rock and water. We see them everywhere, in large and small, in general and particular forms. They are the essential realities of the world and deeply rooted in the world. They come from God, and only God is above them. They oppose one another in hard antagonism at the birth of every thing, whether it be a work of God, of man or of nature. The harsher their conflict, the more distant is a thing from perfection. The more they unite, the closer does every thing approach perfection. When it has reached the highest perfection, the spirit returns to God, and the inert material components destroy one another in the very core of their existence. Heaven and earth perish, and from their ashes the world rises anew. The two forces are renewed and purified, in order to unite and to destroy one another again. We sense this eternal transformation within ourselves, in the world around us, in every lifeless object, and in art.—Man comes into the world helpess, unconscious, at the mercy of fate. Against this terrible menace, maternal love, the highest form of beauty, enters into combat, and unites the wild passions with sweetest love and innocence. At the point of perfection, man recognizes his kinship with the whole world. . . .

When we are carried away by feelings which make our senses tremble to their very depths, we search for concrete symbols which others have found before us, and try to match them to our feeling. In a moment of highest felicity, we may then impart our feeling to others. But if we try to prolong the moment, we overstrain it; the spirit escapes from the borrowed symbol, and we can no longer establish this connection within ourselves, unless we recapture the original intensity of feeling, or become children again. Everybody goes through this cycle in which we suffer recurrent death, and the more often we experience it, the deeper and stronger our feeling becomes. Thus art comes into life and dies, when the spirit has returned to God, leaving only lifeless signs behind.

This sense of our kinship with the whole universe; this jubilant delight of our soul's strongest and most vital spirit; this single chord which strikes every heartstring; this love which holds us and carries us through life; this sweet being besides us, who lives in us and in whose love our soul glows: all these compel and drive us to express ourselves. We hold fast to the peaks of this experience, and this causes certain ideas to arise in us.

We express these ideas in words, sounds, or images, and in this way arouse similar feelings in the hearts of our fellows. All are affected by the truth of this feeling, all feel bound up in this communion, all who feel His presence praise the one and only God, and this causes religion to come into being.—We associate these words, sounds, or images with our strongest feeling, our awareness of God, and with the certain knowledge of our eternal existence which we derive from our sense of coherence with the whole. In other words, we apply these feelings to the most important and vital beings around us, and, by seizing upon the most characteristic traits of these beings, upon those which are most in harmony with our feeling, we create symbols of our thoughts about the world's great forces. . . .

We use these symbols when we want to make others understand great events, beautiful thoughts about nature, and the lovely or terrible sentiments in our soul. . . . We search for events which suit the character of the feelings we want to express, and when we have found them, we have chosen the *subject matter* of art.

When we link this subject with our feeling, we arrange the symbols of natural forces or of our feelings in such a way that they effectively characterize themselves, the subject, and our feeling: this is *composition*.

When we have gained a clear and coherent understanding of the forms of the creatures which we have chosen as our symbols, we can derive their characteristic contour and appearance from their basic essence, from our feeling, and from their natural consistency. We observe their forms in all positions, directions, and expressions, we study every detail of the whole from nature and in relation to the entire composition, the general effect, the particular action, as well as the action of the whole work. We make these forms larger or smaller according to the laws of perspective, study the accessory details and the details of the background in accordance with nature and the subject: and this is *design*.

As we observe the colors of sky and earth, the changes of color produced in human beings by emotions and feelings, the color effects in vast natural phenomena, the relationships and symbolical implications of colors, we give to each object its proper color, establishing its harmony with our original feeling and with the various symbols and objects: this is *coloration*.

We increase or decrease the purity of colors, depending on how close or distant each object is to appear, or how large or small is the volume of air which separates the object from the eye: and this is *value*.

We study the body color of each object and the effect of strong or soft light on it, and of the shadows or lights cast on it by neighboring objects: this is *hue*.

We seek to find the nuances of color which result from the interaction of colored objects and from the fusion of colors through the intervention of light and atmosphere, and we try to determine thoroughly this unifying color key and ultimate accord of our sensations; this is *tone* —and the end.

Art's quest is most beautiful when it issues from and again merges with what is common to all mankind. I want to list here the requirements of a work of art, not merely in the order of their importance, but also in the order in which they must be cultivated by the artist:

1. our awareness of God;
2. our self-awareness in relation to the whole. And, following from these two
3. religion and art, which is the expression of our highest feelings in words, sounds, or images. In the pictorial art, we first look for
4. the subject; then
5. the composition,
6. the design,
7. coloration,

8. value,
9. hue, and
10. tone.

Is it not curious how clearly, how distinctly we sense our life when we watch heavy black clouds rushing past the moon, when we see their edges gilded by the moon or see them swallowing the moon altogether? It then seems to us as if we could write the story of our life in images such as these. And is it not true that since Buonarotti and Raphael there has not been any genuine history paintings? Even Raphael's picture at our gallery [the *Sistine Madonna* in Dresden] approaches landscape—landscape, to be sure, understood in a new way.

[November 7, 1802]

Our delight in flowers comes directly from Paradise. We always associate an inner meaning with flowers, in other words, a human form. And only that is a true flower which we have in mind in our state of joy. When we see our own life reflected in nature, we understand that this is how true landscape art will be realized, as something quite distinct from human action or historical composition.

Flowers, trees, figures will then become intelligible—and we shall have begun to understand color! Color is the ultimate in art. It is still and will always remain a mystery to us, we can only apprehend it intuitively in flowers.—Colors are based on the symbol of Trinity: light or white, black or dark are not colors; light is the good, dark is evil (I am thinking of Creation); we cannot grasp light, and we ought not grasp the dark. Then came the time when man was granted Revelation, and color entered the world: blue, red, and yellow. Light is the sun into which we may not look. But when it descends to the earth and to man, the sky turns red. Blue inspires a certain reverence in us. It is the Father, and red is the Mediator between earth and heaven. When both disappear, then fire lights up the night for us, it is yellow, the Consoler who was sent to us;—the moon, too, is yellow.

William Blake (1757–1827)

In 1809, Blake arranged an exhibition of his "Poetical and Histori-cal Inventions" at the house of his brother, James. Private exhibitions were not uncommon in England, and even on the continent artists, such as David, had recently begun to present their work to the public directly, without submitting to the sponsorship of official bodies (see page 111). Blake's exhibition failed, being "singularly remote from ordinary sym-pathies, or even ordinary apprehensions," in the words of his biographer,

Alexander Gilchrist. Many years after, in 1852, Crabb Robinson remembered having gone to see the "exhibition of Blake's original paintings in Carnaby Market, at a hosier's, Blake's brother. These paintings
filled several rooms of an ordinary dwelling-house, and for the sight, a
half-crown was demanded of the visitor, for which he had a catalogue.
This catalogue I possess, and it is a very curious exposure of the artist's
mind. I wished to send it to Germany and to give a copy to Lamb and
others, so I took four, and giving 10 s., bargained that I should be at
liberty to go again. "Free! as long as you live," said the brother, astonished
at such a liberality, which he had never experienced before, nor I dare
say did afterwards. . . . There were about thirty oil-paintings, the colouring excessively dark and high, the veins black, and the colour of the
primitive men very like that of the Red Indians." [53] The few press
notices of the exhibition were savagely hostile. Leigh Hunt's Examiner
called the catalogue "a farrago of nonsense, unintelligibleness and egre-
gious vanity, the wild effusions of a distempered brain."

The Descriptive Catalogue, which accompanied the exhibition, and
the Public Address, written in 1810 after the fiasco, gave a concise statement of Blake's belief in innate ideas as the source of art, his defense of
clear contour against the "blots & blurs" of the Venetians and Flemings,
and his theory of art's prehistoric beginning. Extravagant though they
seemed, his "wild effusions" expressed ideas current in Blake's time. His
condemnations of colorism and of visual realism simply overstated a
common neoclassical attitude, and his interest in primitive origins paral-
leled that of the sect of the Primitifs in France (see page 136). Blake was
the Winckelmann of a patriarchal antiquity that was no more flagrantly
a figment of the imagination than the Homeric and Ossianic ages in
which his more rational contemporaries believed. There is a general
resemblance, furthermore, between Blake's conception of the imagination and the notion of genius, as it had been formulated by the writers
of the Storm and Stress and, earlier, by Young (see page 71). Yet it was
not quite the same. While these writers had described genius as a vital,
productive power, Blake regarded it as a receptive faculty, comparable to
physical sight in that visions appear to it, but are not made by it. In this
respect, Blake's imagination recalls the God-sent visions which Wackenroder (see Vol. II, p. 21) attributed to artists. But to Blake the imagination
was an abiding capability, not an occasional miracle. He agreed with
Lavater's description of genius as a powerful awareness, a burning
certitude which is present in the consciousness, unexplained and un-

[53] Quoted in R. Kazin (ed.), The Portable Blake, New York, The Viking Press,
Inc., 1955, p. 677; see also Mona Wilson, The Life of William Blake, London, Nonesuch,
1927, p. 210, and Thomas Sadler, Diary, Reminiscences, and Correspondence of Henry
Crabb Robinson, London, Macmillan & Co., Ltd., 1869.

questionable. It was Blake's special happiness that this experience came to him through ready-formed images which did not require further translation. On this point, he differed from Runge who was in other ways his German counterpart.[54]

From A Descriptive Catalogue (1809)

Preface

The eye that can prefer the Colouring of Titian and Rubens to that of Michael Angelo and Raphael, ought to be modest and to doubt its own powers. Connoisseurs talk as if Raphael and Michael Angelo had never seen the colouring of Titian or Correggio: They ought to know that Correggio was born two years before Michael Angelo, and Titian but four years after. Both Raphael and Michael Angelo knew the Venetian, and contemned and rejected all he did with the utmost disdain, as that which is fabricated for the purpose to destroy art.

Mr. B. appeals to the Public, from the judgment of those narrow blinking eyes, that have too long governed art in a dark corner. The eyes of stupid cunning never will be pleased with the work any more than with the look of self-devoting genius. The quarrel of the Florentine with the Venetian is not because he does not understand Drawing, but because he does not understand Colouring. How should he, he who does not know how to draw a hand or a foot, know how to colour it?

Colouring does not depend on where the Colours are put, but on where the lights and darks are put, and all depends on Form or Outline, on where that is put; where that is wrong, the Colouring never can be right; and it is always wrong in Titian and Correggio, Rubens and Rembrandt. Till we get rid of Titian and Correggio, Rubens and Rembrandt, We never shall equal Raphael and Albert Dürer, Michael Angelo, and Julio Romano.

*   *   *

No man can believe that either Homer's Mythology, or Ovid's, were the production of Greece or of Latium; neither will any one believe, that the Greek statues, as they are called, were the invention of Greek Artists; perhaps the Torso is the only original work remaining; all the rest are evidently copies, though fine ones, from greater works of the Asiatic Patriarchs. The Greek Muses are daughters of Mnemosyne, or Memory, and not of Inspiration or Imagination, therefore not authors of such

[54] G. Keynes, *Poetry and Prose of William Blake,* London, Nonesuch, 1927, pp. 778 ff., pp. 795 ff. ("The Ancient Britons"); p. 801 ("The spiritual Preceptor" and "Satan calling up his Legions"); p. 805 ("Ruth").

sublime conceptions. Those wonderful originals seen in my visions, were some of them one hundred feet in height; some were painted as pictures, and some carved as basso relievos, and some as groupes of statues, all containing mythological and recondite meaning, where more is meant than meets the eye.

The connoisseurs and artists who have made objections to Mr. B.'s mode of representing spirits with real bodies, would do well to consider that the Venus, the Minerva, the Jupiter, the Apollo, which they admire in Greek statues are all of them representations of spiritual existences, of Gods immortal, to the mortal perishing organ of sight; and yet they are embodied and organized in solid marble. Mr. B. requires the same latitude, and all is well. The Prophets describe what they saw in Vision as real and existing men, whom they saw with their imaginative and immortal organs; the Apostles the same; the clearer the organ the more distinct the object. A Spirit and a Vision are not, as the modern philosophy supposes, a cloudy vapour, or a nothing: they are organized and minutely articulated beyond all that the mortal and perishing nature can produce. He who does not imagine in stronger and better lineaments, and in stronger and better light than his perishing and mortal eye can see, does not imagine at all. The painter of this work asserts that all his imaginations appear to him infinitely more perfect and more minutely organized than any thing seen by his mortal eye. Spirits are organized men. Moderns wish to draw figures without lines, and with great and heavy shadows; are not shadows more unmeaning than lines, and more heavy? O who can doubt this!

Number V. *The Ancient Britons*

In the last Battle of King Arthur, only Three Britons escaped; these were the Strongest Man, the Beautifullest Man, and the Ugliest Man; these three marched through the field unsubdued, as Gods, and the Sun of Britain set, but shall arise again with tenfold splendor when Arthur shall awake from sleep, and resume his dominion over earth and ocean.

The three general classes of men who are represented by the most Beautiful, the most Strong, and the most Ugly, could not be represented by any historical facts but those of our own country, the Ancient Britons, without violating costume. The Britons (say historians) were naked civilized men, learned, studious, abstruse in thought and contemplation; naked, simple, plain in their acts and manners; wiser than after-ages. They were overwhelmed by brutal arms, all but a small remnant; Strength, Beauty, and Ugliness escaped the wreck, and remain for ever unsubdued, age after age. . . .

The Strong Man represents the human sublime. The Beautiful Man represents the human pathetic, which was in the wars of Eden divided into male and female. The Ugly Man represents the human reason. They were originally one man, who was fourfold; he was self-divided, and his real humanity slain on the stems of generation, and the form of the fourth was like the Son of God. How he became divided is a subject of great sublimity and pathos. The Artist has written it under inspiration, and will, if God please, publish it; it is voluminous, and contains the ancient history of Britain, and the world of Satan and of Adam. . . .

It has been said to the Artist, "take the Apollo for the model of your beautiful Man, and the Hercules for your strong Man, and the Dancing Faun for your Ugly Man." Now he comes to his trial. He knows that what he does is not inferior to the grandest Antiques. Superior they cannot be, for human power cannot go beyond either what he does, or what they have done; it is the gift of God, it is inspiration and vision. He had resolved to emulate those precious remains of antiquity; he has done so and the result you behold; his ideas of strength and beauty have not been greatly different. Poetry as it exists now on earth, in the various remains of ancient authors, Music as it exists in old tunes or melodies, Painting and Sculpture as it exists in the remains of Antiquity and in the works of more modern genius, is Inspiration, and cannot be surpassed; it is perfect and eternal. Milton, Shakespeare, Michael Angelo, Raphael, the finest specimens of Ancient Sculpture and Painting and Architecture, Gothic, Grecian, Hindoo and Egyptian, are the extent of the human mind. The human mind cannot go beyond the gift of God, the Holy Ghost. To suppose that Art can go beyond the finest specimens of Art that are now in the world, is not knowing what Art is; it is being blind to the gifts of the spirit. . . .

The strong Man acts from conscious superiority, and marches on in fearless dependence on the divine decrees, raging with the inspirations of a prophetic mind. The Beautiful Man acts from duty and anxious solicitude for the fates of those for whom he combats. The Ugly Man acts from love of carnage, and delight in the savage barbarities of war, rushing with sportive precipitation into the very jaws of the affrighted enemy.

The Roman Soldiers rolled together in a heap before them: "Like the rolling thing before the whirlwind"; each showed a different character, and a different expression of fear, or revenge, or envy, or blank horror, or amazement, or devout wonder and unresisting awe.

The dead and the dying, Britons naked, mingled with armed Romans, strew the field beneath. Among these the last of the Bards who were capable of attending warlike deeds, is seen falling, outstretched among the dead and the dying, singing to his harp in the pains of death.

Distant among the mountains are Druid Temples, similar to Stone Henge. The Sun sets behind the mountains, bloody with the day of battle.

The flush of health in flesh exposed to the open air, nourished by the spirits of forests and floods in that ancient happy period, which history has recorded, cannot be like the sickly daubs of Titian or Rubens. Where will the copier of nature as it now is, find a civilized man, who is accustomed to go naked? Imagination only can furnish us with colouring appropriate, such as is found in the Frescos of Raphael and Michael Angelo: the disposition of forms always directs colouring in works of true art. As to a modern Man, stripped from his load of cloathing he is like a dead corpse. Hence Reubens, Titian, Correggio and all of that class, are like leather and chalk; their men are like leather, and their women like chalk, for the disposition of their forms will not admit of grand colouring; in Mr. B.'s Britons the blood is seen to circulate in their limbs; he defies competition in colouring.

Number VIII.

The spiritual Preceptor, an experiment Picture.

The subject is taken from the Visions of Emanuel Swedenborg, Universal Theology, No. 623. The Learned, who strive to ascend into Heaven by means of learning, appear to Children like dead horses, when repelled by the celestial spheres. The works of this visionary are well worthy the attention of Painters and Poets; they are foundations for grand things; the reason they have not been more attended to is because corporeal demons have gained a predominance; who the leaders of these are, will be shown below. Unworthy Men who gain fame among Men, continue to govern mankind after death, and in their spiritual bodies oppose the spirits of those who worthily are famous; and, as Swedenborg observes, by entering into disease and excrement, drunkenness and concupiscence, they possess themselves of the bodies of mortal men, and shut the doors of mind and of thought by placing Learning above Inspiration. O Artist! you may disbelieve all this, but it shall be at your own peril.

Number IX.

Satan calling up his Legions, from Milton's Paradise Lost; a composition for a more perfect Picture afterward executed for a Lady of high rank. An experiment Picture.

These Pictures, among numerous others painted for experiment, were the result of temptations and perturbations, labouring to destroy

Imaginative power, by means of that infernal machine called Chiaro Os-
curo, in the hands of Venetian and Flemish Demons, whose enmity to the
Painter himself, and to all Artists who study in the Florentine and Roman
Schools, may be removed by an exhibition and exposure of their vile
tricks. They cause that every thing in art shall become a Machine. They
cause that the execution shall be all blocked up with brown shadows.
They put the original Artist in fear and doubt of his own original conception. The spirit of Titian was particularly active in raising doubts
concerning the possibility of executing without a model, and when once
he had raised the doubt, it became easy for him to snatch away the vision
time after time, for, when the Artist took his pencil to execute his ideas,
his power of imagination weakened so much and darkened, that memory
of nature, and of Pictures of the various schools possessed his mind, instead of appropriate execution resulting from the inventions; like walking
in another man's style, or speaking, or looking in another man's style
and manner, unappropriate and repugnant to your own individual character; tormenting the true Artist, till he leaves the Florentine, and adopts
the Venetian practice, or does as Mr. B. has done, has the courage to
suffer poverty and disgrace, till he ultimately conquers.

Rubens is a most outrageous demon, and by infusing the remem-
brances of his Pictures and style of execution, hinders all power of individual thought: so that the man who is possessed by this demon loses
all admiration of any other Artist but Rubens and those who were his
imitators and journeymen; he causes to the Florentine and Roman
Artist fear to execute; and though the original conception was all fire
and animation, he loads it with hellish brownness, and blocks up all its
gates of light except one, and that one he closes with iron bars, till the
victim is obliged to give up the Florentine and Roman practice and adopt
the Venetian and Flemish.

Correggio is a soft and effeminate, and consequently a most cruel
demon, whose whole delight is to cause endless labour to whoever suffers
him to enter his mind. . . .

Number XV.

Ruth.—A Drawing.

The distinction that is made in modern times between a Painting
and a Drawing proceeds from ignorance of art. The merit of a Picture
is the same as the merit of a Drawing. The dauber daubs his Drawings;
he who draws his Drawings draws his Pictures. There is no difference
between Raphael's Cartoons and his Frescos, or Pictures, except that the
Frescos, or Pictures, are more finished. When Mr. B. formerly painted in
oil colours his Pictures were shown to certain painters and connoisseurs,

who said that they were very admirable Drawings on canvass, but not Pictures; but they said the same of Raphael's Pictures. Mr. B. thought this the greatest of compliments, though it was meant otherwise. If losing and obliterating the outline constitutes a Picture, Mr. B. will never be so foolish as to do one. Such art of losing the outlines is the art of Venice and Flanders; it loses all character, and leaves what some people call expression; but this is a false notion of expression; expression cannot exist without character as its stamina; and neither character nor expression can exist without firm and determinate outline. . . .

The great and golden rule of art, as well as of life, is this: That the more distinct, sharp, and wiry the bounding line, the more perfect the work of art, and the less keen and sharp, the greater is the evidence of weak imitation, plagiarism, and bungling.

From *Public Address* (1810) [55]

Men think they can Copy Nature as Correctly as I copy Imagination; this they will find Impossible, & all the Copies or Pretended Copiers of Nature, from Rembrandt to Reynolds, Prove that Nature becomes to its Victim nothing but Blots & Blurs. Why are Copiers of Nature Incorrect, while Copiers of Imagination are Correct? this is manifest to all.

* * *

The English Artist may be assured that he is doing an injury and injustice to his Country while he studies & imitates the Effects of Nature. England will never rival Italy while we servilely copy what the Wise Italians, Raphael & Michael Angelo, scorned, nay abhorred, as Vasari tells us.

* * *

A Jockey that is anything of a Jockey will never buy a Horse by the Colour, & a Man who has got any brains will never buy a Picture by the Colour.

* * *

No Man of Sense ever supposes that copying from Nature is the Art of Painting: if Art is no more than this, it is no better than any other Manual Labor; anybody may do it & the fool often will do it best as it is a work of no Mind.

[55] G. Keynes, *op. cit.*, pp. 808 ff.

Index